PLANNING YOUR FUTURE

KEYS TO FINANCIAL FREEDOM

Stephen Konowalow, Ph.D.

COMMUNITY COLLEGE OF SOUTHERN NEVADA

Prentice
Hall

Upper Saddle River, New Jersey
Columbus, Ohio

Vice President and Publisher: Jeffery W. Johnston
Senior Acquisitions Editor: Sande Johnson
Assistant Editor: Cecilia Johnson
Production Editor: Holcomb Hathaway
Design Coordinator: Diane C. Lorenzo
Cover Designer: Thomas Borah
Cover Art: Corbis Stock Market
Production Manager: Pamela D. Bennett
Director of Marketing: Ann Castel Davis
Director of Advertising: Kevin Flanagan
Marketing Manager: Christina Quadhamer

This book was set in Sabon by Aerocraft Charter Art Service.
The cover was printed by Phoenix Color Corp.

Pearson Education Ltd.
Pearson Education Australia Pty. Limited
Pearson Education Singapore Pte. Ltd.
Pearson Education North Asia Ltd.
Pearson Education Canada, Ltd.
Pearson Educación de Mexico, S.A. de C.V.
Pearson Education–Japan
Pearson Education Malaysia Pte. Ltd.
Pearson Education, Upper Saddle River, New Jersey

10 9 8 7 6 5
ISBN 0-13-098892-8

Dedication

To my family, who put up with my many absences during the time it took to put this book together: I thank each of you for your support as I brought this book to completion—especially my wonderful and beautiful wife, Kathy, for providing strength for me and for the entire family. Your love, your warmth, and your constructive suggestions never relented and made the challenge all the more worthwhile. Life with you keeps getting better and better.

To my daughters Rhonda, Erika, and Terry; my son Robert; my sisters Fran and Shelley; my brother-in-law Eddie; my friend Bobbie; and the rest of the Konowalow family, I love you all.

To the Eschtruth family, my late father-in-law Lynn Eschtruth, and my mother-in-law Patricia Eschtruth, I thank you for your love, devotion, and support throughout all my ventures.

Lastly, where would I be if I did not remember my parents—my beloved mother and father, Terry and Julius Konowalow? You left me a wonderful legacy of love, compassion, understanding, drive, determination, and a never-quit attitude. In my heart, you are both always with me.

BRIEF CONTENTS

CONTENTS

3

The Best Path to the Best Investments   35

STUDY, STUDY, STUDY!

Discovering Hidden Money   63

 Successful Financial Planning   89

 Financial Freedom   99

BUDGETING AND MEETING YOUR GOALS

ACKNOWLEDGMENTS

I would like to thank the following professional colleagues: Dr. Ron Remington, president, the Community College of Southern Nevada; Dr. Robert Silverman, president of Oregon State College and formerly interim president, the Community College of Southern Nevada; Theo Byrns, interim vice president, Academic Affairs; Thomas Brown, provost and interim vice president, Student Affairs; Dr. Don Smith, dean of Arts and Letters, the Community College of Southern Nevada; Dr. Cynthia Glickman, interim associate dean for distance education; Dr. Robert M. Sherfield, professor, the Community College of Southern Nevada; Dr. Rhonda J. Montgomery, assistant professor, the University of Nevada, Las Vegas; Dr. Patricia G. Moody, dean, the University of South Carolina; Dr. Charles Mosley, department chair, English, the Community College of Southern Nevada; Jim Matovina, professor, the Community College of Southern Nevada; Willie E. Thompson, vice president, Student Affairs, Delta College; and Joe Estrada, director, Webster University, Las Vegas campus.

My sincerest appreciation and gratitude also go to the following professionals, who have permitted me to share with them my ideas about money and money management: Dr. Ron Casey, Joe Niemiec, Al Soprano, Trish LaFlamme, Lynn Forkos, John Kuminecz, Frazine Jasper, Lonnie Wright, Dell Griffin, and Paula Bourne, all of the Community College of Southern Nevada; Ellen Waxman and Evy Wolfgram of Delta College, University Center, Michigan; Jay and Mel Chabrow, Stu Stein, Mort and Sal Friedlander, and Steve and Shelley Aizenberg of Nevada. To Sande L. Johnson, senior acquisitions editor, Cecilia Johnson, assistant editor, both at Prentice Hall, and Gay Pauley, my production editor—where would I be without you? To my dear friend and colleague Robb Sherfield, I offer special thanks for your untiring support of each of my endeavors and for your willingness to let me bore you about the topic of money. To my students—on campus, over TV, Internet, and e-mail, and at the Nevada prisons—I thank you for the many contributions you made as I presented the topic of money, and for your openness to change. The continuing encouragement that I received from these people provided me the support I needed in those moments when I might otherwise have called it quits.

ABOUT THE AUTHOR

Steve Konowalow has been a professional educator, lecturer, writer, author, humorist, and TV and radio personality. He makes it a point to see the abilities and talents in people and the beauty in life. He has spent more than thirty years specializing in the areas of learning enhancement, communication, stress management, organizational development, behavior change, and financial education. Never a financial advisor, Steve finds joy in teaching the art of money management to all who wish to learn.

For almost thirty years, he was with Delta College, a community college in Michigan. There, he earned the rank of full professor and served as a counselor, a professor, the interim chairman of the Applied Behavioral Studies/Study Skills discipline (1974–1992), and the Associate Dean for Student Support Services/Director of Special Student Populations (1993–1994). In August 1995, the Community College of Southern Nevada, Las Vegas, invited him to join the teaching staff as an Instructor of Study Skills, and he accepted the position. He currently teaches in the classroom and via multimedia instruction. He developed the Television Study Skills Distance Education course for instruction via TV, the Internet, and e-mail. His website address is www.solvetd.com. In addition, he holds adjunct professor appointments at the Las Vegas campuses of Webster University, Nova Southwestern University, and the University of Phoenix.

Steve earned a Ph.D. from Wayne State University (Michigan) in Educational Sociology and a B.A. in Sociology from S.U.N.Y. at Buffalo. He also earned an Ed.S. in Student Personnel Administration from Central Michigan University and two master's degrees (M.A. in Higher Education Administration and M.Ed. in Supervision, Community College Administration, and Learning Theory), one from Central Michigan and the other from Duke University.

At Delta College, colleagues nominated Steve five times (1989–1993) for the Outstanding Educators' Recognition Award. At the Community College of Southern Nevada, he was one of the recipients of the UCCSN Regents' Outstanding Faculty 1997–1998 Award and a 1998 and 2000 nominee for the CCSN Outstanding Teaching Faculty Award. Also, he was the editor of both the Nevada Faculty Alliance *Impart* newsletter and the Faculty Center for Learning and Teaching *Beyond the Classroom 1999* and *2000* publications.

Since 1975, Steve has created, designed, and presented programs and seminars to businesses, educational institutions, governmental organizations, hospitals, law enforcement and social service agencies, and industry groups for improving individual and staff relations, management, listening, communication, collaboration, change, organizational development, individual performance, and financial wealth.

Steve is the author of *Cornerstones for Money Management,* published in 1997 by Allyn and Bacon. He has also written two behavioral texts, *Up, Up, and Away* and *Stress Break,* and two motivational tapes. His organizational development and behavior change book, *New Directions to Take Charge: Changing Paradigms, Changing Behaviors, Changing Results,* was published in 1999, and he is currently completing another book, tentatively titled *Opening New Doors: Thinking Outside the Box.* He is also the editor for several publications.

Steve's purpose in life is to make a difference. His focus is on helping individuals and organizations break their cycle of self-limiting thinking so they can maximize their potential; enhance their learning; reduce distress; and experience new levels of achievement, excellence, performance, and financial reward.

A WORD TO THE READER

People of all ages are interested in the topic of money. Unfortunately, many people have distorted views regarding saving money and preparing for retirement, whether they are 18, 20, 25, 45, or 55 years old. Age becomes irrelevant when it comes to saving and investing. For this reason, it is necessary that individuals of all ages become more alert to the issues involved in making their future financially safe, protected, and healthy. Whether you are 15 or 95, you need to know about money, because lack of knowledge about money and money management can be devastating to you during your retirement years.

Planning Your Future: Keys to Financial Freedom focuses on the younger or newer investor, but it also contains information that older or more experienced investors may find enlightening. So, whether you are still in high school, starting college, entering the job market, or about to retire, this book has something for you. The book is not just about *money,* but it is also about *planning, goal setting,* and *creating a financially secure future* for yourself and your family.

This book takes the novice investor through the steps to achieve financial success today and tomorrow. For the mature and experienced investor, it presents success keys—new ways of doing things financially.

As an educator, I find that one area that has been overlooked at all levels of schooling is the study of money—understanding it, saving it, keeping it, investing it, and having it for the future. You may not think about retirement, but in fact your retirement will depend upon what you do today to save for your nonworking years.

Many educational environments teach a curriculum covering accounting, banking, economics, and finance. These are all wonderful subjects, but they do not specifically address money concerns for the teenage through retirement years or the basics and intricacies of becoming financially successful and independent.

If you think you are too young or too old to benefit from this book, you are wrong. Please do not pick up this book and say, "I am just in high school or just beginning college. I don't have to consider my financial future for the next 10 or 20 years." You would be wrong! Please do not think that you are too old and say, "It is too late—I am almost 50. I don't have enough time to learn about money or even to invest what I have." Wrong, again!

The literature attests to the fact that people who retire today at 55, 60, or 65 will in all probability live another 30 or more years. In coming decades, life expectancy beyond retirement will continue to increase. Simple mathematics indicates that you need to learn to make money plans today, so you can have it tomorrow.

One statistic I find scary is that more than 50% of working men and women aged 55 and older do not have a retirement plan. Nor have these people set aside funds for retirement, except for Social Security. As you will learn, Social Security is not sufficient for living expenses in your nonworking years.

The focus of this book is how to prepare for your financial future. Applying the simple strategies this book provides will not only help you understand money, but also save it and keep it. If you are to be a successful investor, you need to read about money and understand it. You need to identify your dreams, your goals, and your plans, and how you deal with money.

Through the pages of this book, you will be guided via a variety of **KEYS** (think of them as keys to a treasure chest) to help you get started, learn the terminology, and develop a financial plan. Pay particular attention to the **KEYS**. These **KEYS** give quick informational tips about financial success.

 Your first **KEY**: *Do not depend on others for your financial success.* You must learn to do this yourself. There are *no* financial gurus. I do not claim to be a financial guru or a financial advisor. Instead, I see myself as a financial educator. I teach that the best way to know about money and money management is to study it. Learn the terminology. Study the market and the investment funds available. Study, study, and study! If you don't know what funds are out there, make it a point to find out about them. Financial decisions take planning. So, besides studying, you must be willing to plan. You must also be willing to accept some changes in the way you think about money. To be successful at investing, you may well need to change many of your ideas about money. You must accept the fact that investing takes not only study, but time as well. You must be willing to give your money the time to grow.

The ideas in this book can show you how to succeed. You will learn the difference between making a choice and taking a chance, about credit and how much credit you need. You will also learn that there are pitfalls to having a credit card and debt. You will be introduced to government savings programs designed to help you set up your own retirement plan. These programs can help you become financially secure, but only if you take advantage of the opportunity and do so early. You will also learn the value of education—the more the better. There is a section devoted to how to keep the money that you save today safe for tomorrow—for you in your retirement years and, if you desire, for your children. There is also a section on wills and probate.

Planning Your Future provides realistic ideas about money and the art of managing it, and a clear explanation of the road to financial security.

KEY: *Planning for your future and retirement years must begin today.*

GETTING STARTED
SETTING GOALS, CREATING THE DREAM

Why Do I Need to Know About Money? I Have Time . . .

Most people think they have all the time in the world to invest, to plan for their future, and to set aside money for their retirement. For most people, this is not entirely correct.

If you are able to read this book and you have not already begun to set aside money in a retirement plan that invests funds regularly—at least on a monthly basis—you may be running out of time. I do not mean to scare you, but to make you aware that in the world of investing, the time needed to see growth requires 20, 40, or even 60 years. You need to think about the future now, so you can set appropriate goals to meet your financial needs at retirement. Let's face it: Although many people work beyond 65 into their 70s or 80s, many others decide to retire or semiretire by 62 or 65.

No more excuses. No more procrastinating. Now is the time to get started on setting up a financial plan and financial goals for your future nonworking years.

Your situation is ideal if, by the time you retire, you will have been putting money away for 60 or more years. However, many of us begin investing late, leaving only 30 to 40 years, or worse, only 10 to 20 years. In such cases, it is still possible to acquire enough capital and savings to retire comfortably, but you will need to do some catching up.

Money plays a powerful role in our lives. It influences your relationships with your spouse, your children, and others with whom you associate. As we all realize, and as research indicates, it even has an effect on your stress level and communication with others. Consequently, it is

crucial that you learn early in life how to discipline yourself in handling this necessary commodity.

Since the first human communities, people have devised ways to acquire possessions through the exchange of goods for service, bartering, and the exchange of one item for another. Before there were currencies as we know them today, people used gold, silver, precious stones, and a variety of trinkets. Do you remember the story of the purchase of the island of Manhattan for $24-worth of beads? Regardless of the time or place, money and its accumulation of it have been of interest to most people.

Most people in the world think or worry about money on a daily basis. There are radio and television programs totally devoted to the topic of money and related issues. Squabbles about and mismanagement of money can result in divisions within families. Divorces may occur over money, and often stipulated in the divorce decree is how the couple's property and assets are to be divided.

People hold a wide range of attitudes toward money. Some believe having money is bad and can only lead to trouble. Others think that money is great and seek out ways to obtain large amounts of it.

What do you think about money? On the lines that follow, write a few of your thoughts on the topic of money.

_____

_____

_____

_____

_____

What did you write? Did you write "money is the root of all evil," or something like "I can never have enough of it"? How about, "money burns a hole in my pocket," or "money is something to spend, share, or give away"? Did you write "money is not very important to me" or "money is a means of security and/or insurance for the future—my future"? You may have written "money is something very difficult to keep," "a measure of one's worth in the world," or "a way of impressing and/or proving oneself to others." Still, you may have written "money is a means for buying freedom," "a way to feel superior," or "a means to buy love."

There is no right or wrong answer when it comes to opinions about money. However, it is true that your financial success will depend upon your ability to manage it, save it, and invest it. Failure to handle money properly may lead to trouble and unhappiness. **KEY:** *Money will not make you happy—only you can do that for yourself. Money does give you the freedom and opportunity to find out what things you enjoy, and this could bring you some degree of happiness.*

Controlling your finances is a simple matter; it is not as hard as some may want you to believe. It will take some discipline and practice, but it is something that can be done. It is important that you make it a point to do it.

KEY: *It is necessary that you make the time to plan.* Will you? Will you sit down and create a budget—that is, a *plan*—so you can see where you stand financially? It is not something that you can put off until later. You can't procrastinate about this. You need to do it, now.

The years go by quickly, and before you know it you are approaching retirement without any funds to enjoy it. Don't be like so many—young and old—who wonder and ask the question: Where did all the money go?

So where does all the money go? This question is not hard to answer. To find out where your money goes, simply keep track of your personal cash income and outgo on a weekly, monthly, and yearly basis. How much do you spend for mortgage/rent, utilities, taxes, loans, food, automobile/gas, social activities, drinking, partying, insurance, medical/dental insurance, and so on? How much did you put in savings or invest?

Looking at your lists, are there costly activities that could be eliminated? Are there activities you could add that are free or inexpensive? You don't want to live a hermit's existence, but even the richest people in the world live on a budget. The secret to financial independence and security includes your willingness to maintain a budget. There it is: that horrible word "budget."

There is a secret to achieving all your ambitions and dreams and helping realize your financial goals. It can become your key to financial success, security, and independence. The secret is that you must plan! **KEY:** *A budget is a financial plan.* This is a simple idea. Some secret, you may be thinking. However, it must be a secret. If it isn't, why aren't people doing it?

Answer the following question: What is a budget?

exercise

_____

_____

_____

Did you answer that a budget is a financial plan to guide you in achieving financial security and independence? Are you aware that the richer you are, the more time you need to invest in planning how to keep your wealth? You can learn to achieve great wealth by doing what the wealthy do: plan. You can accomplish little without a plan. **KEY:** *The secret is to plan.*

Here is a fun assignment on the Internet, go to a savings calculator. Such a calculator can be found at http://cgi.money.cnn.com/tools/moneygrow/ moneygrow_101.html. When the savings calculator comes up, record in the boxes the following numbers. For the Initial Deposit, leave the dollar amount as zero. For the Interest Rate, put in 12% per year, or any percent you select (anything between 8% and 13% would be reasonable). In the Additional Deposits box, type in $180 per year, and lastly, in the How Long You'll Save Box, put 65 years. Record the result here: $_____.

Were you surprised at how much money you would have? Did you notice that it did not take much money to achieve this amount? Just divide $180 by 12. This comes to $15 per month. How often do you throw away $15 in a month, a week, or even a day? **KEY:** *Begin today to save and invest for retirement from birth.* Of course, this may not be possible for you, but when you have children or grandchildren (or if you do), help them start a retirement fund by setting up an account for each of them. The account can be in your name, so you keep the control, or you can make it a joint account with both your names on it.

In this account, you set aside $180 per year. When your child or grand-child reaches 18, you can gift it to him or her. A condition for this gift is that it is unavailable for use until he is 65 years of age or older. Instead, he must put in $180 each year for the next 46 years. When he understands the amount of money that will accrue in savings for having put away only $8,280, he will definitely appreciate your foresight in establishing the account. Using 10% as an annual rate of interest, this account, after 18 years, will be worth to the recipient around $10,000. At that same rate of return, the additional contributions of $180 per year for an additional 46 years will bring the value of the account to near $900,000. This is a very good return on a contribution totaling $11,700. **KEY:** *Time, compound interest, and regular monthly investing pay off in dividends.*

Financial Planning Is a Necessity for All People

A financial plan is not a luxury only for the rich and famous. A financial plan is important for all. **KEY:** *If one wishes to live their retirement years with some degree of comfort and dignity, a financial plan becomes a necessity—a key to financial freedom.*

Know your current financial situation and plan. Fill in Exhibit 1.1, Brief Monthly Financial Statement Worksheet, to get a better understanding of

BRIEF MONTHLY FINANCIAL STATEMENT WORKSHEET.	EXHIBIT 1.1

AS OF (Date)

ASSETS (Amount IN)	$ AMOUNT	LIABILITIES (Amount OUT)	$ AMOUNT
Monthly Taxable Income		Rent/Mortgage	
Cash in Pocket		Utilities — Gas/Electric	
Savings — All Sources/Locations		Phone(s)	
Money in Bank Account(s)		Internet and Cable TV	
Other Assets:		Grocery/Food/Cleaning Stuff	
		Credit Cards	
		Loans	
		Insurances	
		Snacks	
		Junk Food	
		Eating Out	
		Gas for Car	
		Unplanned Activities	
TOTAL ASSETS		TOTAL EXPENSES/LIABILITIES	
		TOTAL ASSETS	
		LESS MONTHLY LIABILITIES	
		AMOUNT LEFT FOR INVESTING	

where you stand at this moment, financially. This will give you insight into your money in and money out.

What did you learn about your money in as compared to your money out? Did you have any money left for investing? If you did, that's a positive outcome. If, however, you found yourself with zero dollars or a negative balance, what are you to do?

If you have no cash beyond your expenses, don't be frustrated. You are among the more than 70% of the U. S. population who live from paycheck to paycheck and say they do not know how they will save, let alone have anything left to invest for retirement. **KEY:** *Be honest with yourself. No more lying about your money!*

You need to avoid lying to yourself about your finances. You know that what you are telling yourself is not true and that it works only temporarily to get you off the hook. The fact is that people who have money have made a choice to spend less. **KEY:** *Avoid spending more than you earn.*

How and where do you waste your money? The monthly financial statement you completed included in the liabilities column several entries on which you could be "wasting" money. Later in this text, we'll talk about *enticers*, which tend to rob you of cash that could be used for savings and investing. Take a moment to complete the following exercise to identify the ways you tend to waste the most money.

The five ways I tend to waste money are:

_____

_____

_____

_____

_____

The money wasting methods you listed may only cost you $1.00 here and $2.00 there, but even this adds up to $3.00 per day. Previously, you saw what could happen if you invested only $180 each year for 65 years. If you did the assignment, you were probably amazed at the result.

You will be equally surprised to see how much saving $3.00 a day can generate. It adds up to a very large sum of money. Don't believe me? The exercise below will allow you to calculate what happens to $3.00 per day when this amount is put away on a daily basis for 40 years at an annual return of 10% interest. I selected $3.00 because that is what most people are willing to admit they "blow" or "waste" on a daily basis. Some people admit to wasting double and triple that amount. How about you? Is $3.00 per day about what you waste? Do you waste more? Or less?

Let's assume that $3.00 each day is in fact what you waste. Now, let's do the exercise. You will need to go back to the savings calculator at http://cgi.money.cnn.com/tools/moneygrow/moneygrow_101.html/. Then place $3.00 in the Initial Deposit box and $3.00 per day in the Additional Deposit box. Put 40 years in the Time box at 10% for the Annual Interest Rate. When you click on the calculate button, you get $586,735.69. Does this surprise you?

Even *you,* by not wasting $3.00 a day, can accumulate over half-a-million dollars in your retirement account. That is only $90 monthly. What would happen if you set aside $120, $160, or $200 each month? (Later in this book, we'll explore investments that allow you to put money away in nontaxable programs, from which you can withdraw every penny without having to pay any federal taxes. Imagine, having more than $500,000 and not paying any taxes. Some of you may live in a state where there is no state tax, either. We live in a wonderful country!)

You do not have to be born into wealth—although it can help—to achieve great wealth. Continue reading, and you will learn the various methods and strategies for achieving your financial dreams.

Using the lines below, write a paragraph summarizing three or more things you learned from this section.

_____

_____

_____

_____

_____

_____

_____

_____

_____

_____

_____

_____

Procrastination: Why Financial Plans Fail

Are you aware that many financial plans fail? Are you equally aware that financial plans that fail most often do so because of procrastination? This is correct. Many people put off financial planning. They tell themselves that they will do it next week, next year, or after they graduate from high school or college. Some say that they will do it after paying off their car. Others say that they are not ready because they do not have the money now. Procrastination only works against you. You need to take action, now.

By planning your finances today, you can set the stage for having a secure financial future tomorrow. To live comfortably in your nonworking years, you will need a financial cushion, and this comes about only through planning.

Unfortunately, many have not planned. As sad as it may seem, it is a fact. The Department of Aging found that 50% of men and 66% of women 55 years of age and older do not have any retirement funds set aside. They have no plan. Instead, they expect Social Security to provide for them and their families in their later years. As I stated previously, Social Security may provide a small stipend, but it will not be enough to live on.

You may say or think: "Big deal. I can work another 5, 7, or 10 years to put away the money I will need for retirement." Unfortunately, saving wisely depends on long-term thinking, investing, and planning. So, procrastination does not work.

Exhibit 1.2 reveals the result of consistent saving/investing in tax-deferred (that is, 401 tax-free) stock mutual funds. (More will be discussed regarding "401 tax-free" and "taxable" investments in Chapter 3.) Exhibit

EXHIBIT 1.2	**$100 CONTRIBUTED MONTHLY INTO TAX-DEFERRED STOCK MUTUAL FUNDS AT VARIOUS RATES OF INTEREST AND ALLOWED TO COMPOUND FOR 5 TO 40 YEARS.**				
INTEREST RATE	**5 YEARS**	**10 YEARS**	**20 YEARS**	**30 YEARS**	**40 YEARS**
3	6,464	13,974	32,830	58,273	92,605
4	6,629	14,724	36,677	69,404	118,196
5	6,800	15,528	41,103	83,225	152,602
6	6,977	16,387	46,204	100,451	199,149
7	7,159	17,308	52,092	121,997	262,481
8	7,347	18,294	58,902	149,035	349,100
9	7,542	19,351	66,788	183,074	468,132
10	7,743	20,484	75,936	226,048	632,407
11	7,951	21,699	86,563	280,451	860,012
12	8,166	23,003	98,925	349,496	1,176,477
13	8,389	24,403	113,324	437,326	1,617,906
14	8,619	25,906	130,116	549,297	2,235,438
15	8,857	27,521	149,723	692,327	3,101,605

Source: Calculated using CNNMoney's *Quick Savings Calculator.* Retrieved online at http://cgi.money.cnn.com/tools/moneygrow/moneygrow_101.html.

1.2 shows, for instance, that a person who put aside $100 for 12 months (that is, $1,200 per year) would accumulate a retirement nest egg of over $500,000, saving for 30 years in funds paying an average of 14%. (Funds with returns as high as 14% are hard to find. It may be more realistic to expect an average return of 9% and 10%.)

Referring to the Exhibit 1.2, how many years would it take you to achieve approximately a $500,000 retirement nest egg at an annual return rate of 9%?

If you read the chart correctly, you observed that it will take you 40 years to achieve $468,132 at 9% interest and $632,407 at 10% interest. If you invested for 40 years and were able to find funds earning between 11% and 12% return on your investment, your retirement savings could exceed $1,000,000. Of course, finding stock mutual funds paying 11% and higher does take work. The secret is to plan and not to procrastinate.
KEY: *Avoid procrastinating!*
What are the consequences of delaying investment, starting later in life to create a retirement fund? Exhibit 1.3 illustrates the cost of procrastina-

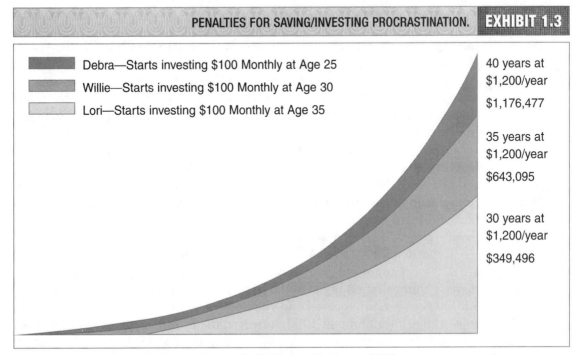

PENALTIES FOR SAVING/INVESTING PROCRASTINATION. **EXHIBIT 1.3**

Debra—Starts investing $100 Monthly at Age 25
Willie—Starts investing $100 Monthly at Age 30
Lori—Starts investing $100 Monthly at Age 35

40 years at $1,200/year
$1,176,477

35 years at $1,200/year
$643,095

30 years at $1,200/year
$349,496

Source: Adapted from a graph in *Z403b News,* Templeton Franklin Investment Services, April 1996.

tion. Study the chart to learn about the investment behavior of Debra, Willie, and Lori, all employed by the same company. Each decided to begin investing at a different time in their employment life. It was not much of a difference in time—as little as 10 years. But it made a great difference in dollars earned in their investment portfolios.

Debra began contributing $1,200 per year when she was 25 years old and made regular monthly contributions for the next 40 years. Willie began at 30 and contributed $1,200 per year in monthly contributions for the next 35 years. The last was Lori. She did not get into the investment mode until she was 35, but she managed to make contributions of $1,200 per year on a regular monthly basis for the next 30 years. Note in Exhibit 1.3 the degree to which a procrastination of 5 years can set back a retirement nest egg.

KEY: *Investing is a long-term proposition, requiring commitment. Don't wait!*

The Problem with Waiting Too Long and Running Out of Time

Let's take a moment to look at the situation of a person who is 55 years of age, has not planned for retirement other than counting on Social Security, and has no nest egg set aside. Many people in this situation will tell you that they can put away money for the next 5, 7, or 10 years because they plan to work until they are 65. How realistic is such a plan?

KEY: *Make it a point to invest regularly. Do not leave your retirement to your last 10 years of employment.* You must plan today for your financial security tomorrow. For maximum income from retirement funds, it is best to put money away for 30, 35, or 40 years. Starting late is better than not starting at all, however. There is good news, even for late starters.

The laws have changed. Have you ever heard of IRAs (Individual Retirement Accounts)? There are two kinds: traditional and Roth. Later, you will learn about their differences. For now, we'll focus on how your money grows in an IRA account. It is the same for both.

To participate in an IRA, you need to be working. The only restrictions are that you cannot put away more than you earned in a given year and that there is a prespecified limit. In the past, you could put away only a total of $2,000 per year, for yourself and your spouse (assuming that you were both working). Beginning in 2002, however, the limit increased—to $3,000— and it will eventually rise to $4,000 and then $5,000 per year, for each of you. If your spouse is not working, there are other rules to consid-

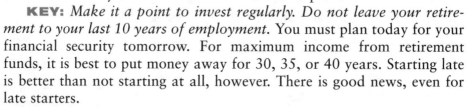

er, and if you had no income during the year, you will need to look for other investment vehicles. Don't worry; there are many.

Exhibit 1.4 shows what happens over time to money invested in an IRA on a monthly basis. There are three scenarios. In the first example, a person makes contributions of $83 per month—$996 per year. The second person contributes $165 per month, a total yearly contribution of $1,980. The third person makes a contribution of $415 per month, or $4,980 per year. The point of Exhibit 1.4 is to show that there are considerable penalties if you start to invest late.

People who leave only 5, 7, or 10 years to invest for their retirement will fall considerably short of achieving the $500,000 nest egg goal. On the other hand, as you study the chart, you can see that starting early and making a lifetime commitment to investing can turn even a humble investor into a millionaire and some into multimillionaires over a 40-year period. However, notice that over a 10-year period, even if you put away almost $5,000 each year, you can reach only around $95,000 in your retirement fund—and that assumes an annual rate of return of 12%. To reach $500,000 in a 10-year period, you would need to make monthly contributions of $2,175, or $26,100 per year. Besides being a lot of money, it is well outside the limit of either of the two current IRA programs' allowable contribution. It is even more unrealistic to set aside monthly contributions for only 5 or 7 years. To achieve $500,000 in 5 years, it would be necessary to invest $6,100 per month; for 7 years, it would be necessary to invest $3,800 per month. How many people do you know who can put $73,200 or $45,600, respectively, into savings each year? Begin early: it makes the goal much easier.

| MONTHLY CONTRIBUTIONS TO A NONSPECIFIED IRA FROM 5 YEARS TO 40 YEARS AT AN AVERAGE ANNUAL RATE OF RETURN OF 12%. | | | | | | **EXHIBIT 1.4** |

AMOUNT OF CONTRIBUTION MONTHLY	YEARLY	5 YEARS	7 YEARS	10 YEARS	25 YEARS	40 YEARS
183	996	6,778	10,845	19,093	155,944	976,476
165	1,980	13,475	21,560	37,956	310,009	1,941,187
250	3,000	20,417	32,668	57,509	469,711	2,941,193
330	3,960	26,950	43,121	75,912	620,019	3,882,374
415	4,980	33,892	54,228	95,466	779,721	4,882,380

Using the lines below, write a paragraph summarizing three or more things you learned from this section.

_____

_____

_____

_____

_____

_____

_____

_____

Dreaming: Taking the First Step to Creating a Financial Plan

A plan begins with a dream. Psychologically, dreaming is healthy. Think for a second about your dreams. Perhaps they are graduating from college; having a family, career, children, grandchildren, or a new home; living past 90; retiring; or achieving financial success. Take a moment to fill out the financial dream exercise on the following page.

MAKING YOUR FINANCIAL DREAM COME TRUE   Part One

My financial plan/goal is to:

_____

_____

State your goal clearly, as well as when you want to have achieved it. Give yourself a definite target date.

I plan to have my financial plan/goal achieved on [day/month/year]:

day _____ *month* _____ *year* _____ *at (time)* _____

Be honest with yourself. Think about the cost and loss. What would the cost and loss be if you did not achieve your financial goal?

If I do not attain my financial goal, I would experience the following costs and losses:

_____

_____

_____

_____

_____

Can you accept these?   ❑ Yes   ❑ No   [*If this is a true goal, the answer should be "no."*] *Next, consider the gains associated with achieving your financial goal.*

The gains that I would experience for achieving my financial goal are:

_____

_____

_____

_____

_____

Don't the gains make the financial goal even more desirable?   ❑ Yes   ❑ No

Your financial success begins with a dream. What is your financial dream? Close your eyes and attempt to visualize achieving that dream. Write it out again. Don't be shy. Nobody but you will see this, unless you choose otherwise.

_____

_____

_____

_____

_____

Did what you wrote above change from what you had written on the previous page? This is not unusual. Keep redefining your dream. Dreaming is healthy because it helps you make plans and achieve goals.

On the previous page, you were asked to write a goal. A goal has six criteria: (1) it is believable, (2) it is reasonable, (3) it is achievable by your own talents and abilities, (4) it can be accomplished within a specific time-line, (5) it is adjustable and controllable, and (6) it is something you desire. The last point—*desirable*—is very important. It means that any thought of not accomplishing your goal is unacceptable. Go back and re-examine your financial goal/plan. Does it meet all the above criteria? Does it need to be revised? Using the financial dream exercise on the next page, revise your goal.

Don't be surprised if you rewrite and revise your goal/plan often. Getting the dream clearly planted in your mind will help you remember what it is you want to accomplish.

Now that you've revised your plan, does it seem closer to what you want? Knowing your financial goal will help you achieve your financial plan and gain success and independence. It will take some effort on your part, but the results will be well worth it.

MAKING YOUR FINANCIAL DREAM COME TRUE   Part Two

My financial plan/goal is to:

_____

_____

State your goal clearly, as well as when you want to have achieved it. Give yourself a definite target date.

I plan to have my financial plan/goal achieved on [day/month/year]:

*day*_____*month*_____*year*_____*at (time)*_____

Be honest with yourself. Think about the cost and loss. What would the cost and loss be if you did not achieve your financial goal?

If I do not attain my financial goal, I would experience the following costs and losses:

_____

_____

_____

_____

_____

Can you accept these?   ❏ Yes   ❏ No   [*If this is a true goal, the answer should be "no."*] *Next, consider the gains associated with achieving your financial goal.*

The gains that I would experience for achieving my financial goal are:

_____

_____

_____

_____

_____

Don't the gains make the financial goal even more desirable?   ❏ Yes   ❏ No

TREASURE CHEST

Using the lines below, write a short summary of what you learned as a result of reading this chapter. Make it a point to list at least *three* **KEYS** in your writing. Indicate clearly how you expect to use these **KEYS** to guide your financial life.

_____

_____

_____

_____

_____

_____

_____

_____

_____

_____

_____

_____

_____

_____

_____

_____

_____

_____

_____

_____

_____

2

BECOMING FINANCIALLY INDEPENDENT

How would you define financial independence? Do you have a dollar amount in mind? In Chapter 1, I suggested that to retire comfortably today you would need approximately $500,000 in a retirement fund. That may sound like a lot of money. But for some people, it may be only 10% of what they plan to have in their retirement fund. Can you imagine a retirement fund balance of $5,000,000 or $10,000,000? It is not impossible. It just takes planning. With planning, you can have all that you need and more.

Key to Financial Independence: Spend Less

The key to building financial independence sounds so simple: Spend less than you make. Yet, many people spend more than they make, and they do this on a regular basis. Are you living beyond your income? What did you learn about your expenditures when you completed the Brief Monthly Statement Worksheet (Exhibit 1.1)? Did you learn that you have too much credit card debt, that you have little to no cash, or that your paycheck doesn't meet your minimum monthly financial necessities?

To repeat the major theme of Chapter 1, *now* is the time to plan for your financial future. It does not matter how old you are—the important thing is that you begin *now* to put your finances in order. Using the agreement below, set down your retirement savings goals, as the first step in developing an investment plan. **KEY:** *Begin now to put money in your savings/investment fund first.* That's right—you now come first. All your other bills are paid *after* you have paid yourself. This means that you must spend less than you are currently spending to have enough income to cover all your expenses *and* your #1 priority—a payment to your retirement fund.

An Agreement of Understanding with Myself

My goal is to save the following amount of money each month: $ _____. By not wasting this money, I will have $ _____ at the end of each month. My goal is to save/invest $ _____ per year for the next _____ years. My nest egg goal is $ _____.

Signed by: _____ Date _____

It is up to you to honor your agreement and to achieve each of your stated goals. You and you alone are the single most important factor in your own success. Besides learning to pay yourself first the amount you have decided you need, learn why you need to save for retirement and how to optimize your investments.

Using the lines below, write a paragraph summarizing three or more things that you learned from this section.

_____

_____

_____

_____

_____

_____

The Need to Save for Retirement

How much money will you need in your retirement years? The goal is to have a nest egg of about $500,000, but with inflation, $1,000,000 or more would be preferable. Begin now, and you can easily set aside that amount over the next 30, 35, or 40 years. It does not matter whether you are from a wealthy family. Anyone can achieve wealth with consistent planning and regular monthly contributions to a retirement program.

Although it may be difficult for you to think about saving or investing money today, it is a necessity. Having income tomorrow requires putting away money now. Whether you want to admit it, you will not work forever. Wouldn't your retirement years be brighter if you were financially secure?

The Expectation: You Will Live
20 Years Beyond Retirement

Are you in good health, today?   ❏ Yes   ❏ No

Do you expect to be in good health when you retire?   ❏ Yes   ❏ No

The prognosis is good for you—whether male or female—to live more than 20 years beyond retirement. Research into life expectancy shows that people retiring at 65 today can expect to live another 25 years or more. This means that if you have a fairly risk-free lifestyle, take care of yourself, and have good genes, you could live to be 90, 100, or even older.

One study, the "Grandfather Economic Heath Care Report," found that men who were 65 years old in 2000 could expect to live another 16 years, to age 81; women could expect to live another 19 years, to age 84 (http://home.att.net/~mwhodges/healthcare.htm). Other reports show these numbers to be low, so it gets better. The conclusions of a study done by the Life Insurance Research Center at *QuickQuote* are shown in Exhibit 2.1.

Exhibit 2.1 shows that a 65-year-old male has a 50% chance of living another 21 years and 50% of females 65 years of age can expect to live anoth-

LIFE EXPECTANCY CHART, UNITED STATES.   EXHIBIT 2.1

GENDER	CURRENT AGE	50% WILL LIVE TO
Male	60	85
	65	86
	70	87
	75	89
	80	91
	85	93
Female	60	89
	65	90
	70	90
	75	91
	80	93
	85	94

Source: Data from Life Insurance Resource Center (2001). *QuickQuote Financial Inc.* Retrieved online at www.quickquote.com/lires.html/, December 2, 2001.

er 25 years. Using the information from Exhibit 2.1 and combining it with a report from the National Education Association, we learn that of men and women aged 65 in 1940, only 7.4% had a life expectancy of 90, but by 1980, 24.4% of a similar population could expect to live to 90. If we project further using this data, 50% of people who were 65 in 2000 have a life expectancy of about 90 (see Exhibit 2.2). Because the percentage of people projected to live beyond 90 keeps increasing, it would not be surprising if more than 50% of the men and women who reach 65 in 2040 lived beyond 90 years of age.

Today, the possibility for you to live 25, 30, or more years beyond your retirement is more a reality than ever before. The reality of longer life beyond retirement raises a question: Assuming you live 25 to 30 years after you stop working, how will you support yourself? If you are married, how will you ensure that your family has sufficient income to enjoy these years? Where will your money come from, if you can only expect a small amount from Social Security? The answer is *planning*. Now is the time to formulate a plan to make those years enjoyable. You must plan today to have money in retirement for tomorrow.

Perhaps you don't believe that you will live to age 90 or even close to it. If interested, you can actually determine your life expectancy. Knowing this

EXHIBIT 2.2   PERCENTAGE OF MEN AND WOMEN EXPECTED TO LIVE TO 90, UNITED STATES.

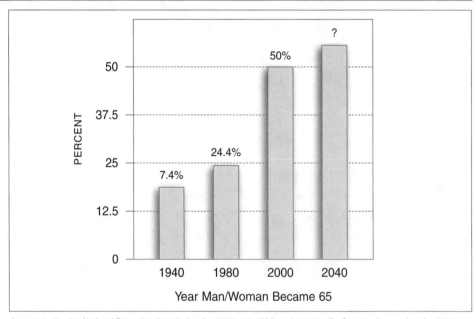

As reported by the National Education Association for 1940 and 1980, projected by Dr. Stephen Konowalow for 2000 and 2040.

information will certainly motivate you more to plan for your retirement. To find out how close to 100 you can expect to live, bring up the life calculator site at the following URL: http://geography.miningco.com/cs/lifeexpectancy/. Click on the Living to 100 Life Expectancy Calculator link and do the exercise. You may be surprised at how much time you can expect after retirement.

Whatever the answer, you are likely to live beyond 65 years of age, and neither your employer nor the government can provide all the money you will need in your nonworking years. This is *your* responsibility.

The Department of Labor reports that the average male and female (married or unmarried, but without children) works approximately 37.5 years. The married female or a female with children works approximately 30 years. This means that you can expect to be retired for as long as you have worked, and possibly longer. When you make the decision to retire, you need to know how you will fund the next 30 and more years of your and your family's life. Again, you are responsible for the results.

Whether you are male or female, assume that you will work only until you are 65. In the ensuing years, how will you support yourself and, if relevant, your family? One tends to assume that children would be grown by then and be living on their own. This may not be an accurate assumption in today's world, however.

Around 30 years ago, a trend toward parenting at an older age became recognized. Since the 1970s, many more men and women have had children at older ages, even 40 and 50. It is, therefore, more possible than it used to be that children will still be at home when their parents retire.

Moreover, health research reports that working tends to promote health and longer lives. As an octogenarian acquaintance related to me, "Work is what keeps me young and alive." The late George Burns, who died when he was over 100, showed that although the body may slow down, the mind becomes sharper with age. Retired men and women are active and busy. Research also demonstrates a strong relationship between living longer and having set aside a retirement fund.

Using the lines below, write a paragraph summarizing three or more things you learned from this section.

exercise

_____

_____

_____

_____

Optimizing Your Investment: Taking Advantage of Time, Savings, and Compound Interest

The environment of money management is changing quickly. You will be at an advantage if you know how to be part of this change. Generally held expectations about work and retirement are gone—no longer true: One does not work at one job until retirement; employers no longer provide employees with a full retirement package; and Social Security does not provide an adequate income in retirement. Also, many people are retiring before 65 or even before they reach 62.

KEY: *Get started saving and investing early.* The earlier you start investing in your retirement, the more you will accumulate and the more comfortably you can expect to live in the future. Accumulating wealth has to do with the amount set aside for saving, the time for it to grow, and the rate of interest on your investment. Savings, time, and compound interest will have an immense effect upon your future wealth. Because time counts and keeps on counting, learn how to use time to your advantage by making

now a solid financial plan for your future. **KEY:** *The key to your financial success will be your willingness to start planning early and to follow through with that plan.*

Think for a moment. If you want to remember your daily schedule, you maintain a calendar—a plan. If you want to take a trip, you make a travel plan. If you want to run a business, you develop a business plan. In all areas of your life, planning is a major component of success.

Financial success and security result from continuous financial planning. Although it may sound extreme, financial planning must begin at birth and

can only end with your death. **KEY:** *Financial planning is a lifelong commitment.* This is why you cannot wait to develop the skills needed to become financially independent and secure.

Using the lines below, write a paragraph summarizing three or more things you learned from this section.

_____

_____

_____

_____

_____

There Are No Gurus: You Are Responsible for Your Success

The New York Stock Exchange is referred to as "the market." Investors watch the market—watch it go up, hopefully. The three big indexes are the Dow, the Nasdaq, and the S&P. These indexes can also go down, and they do. What the market or indexes do in a day, a week, a month, or even a year, however, does not have much of a bearing on your investments. This is because in the investment world, the timeframe is decades for seeing money double, triple, and quadruple.

Peter Lynch, vice chairman of Fidelity Investments and former portfolio manager of the Fidelity Magellan Fund, stated in an article at www.fidelity.com that "the market has historically been volatile with declines of over 10% 21 times and over 20% eight times since 1970. . . ." Yet in spite of these declines the market has continued to bounce back and to rise, and will do so again and again.

Warren Buffett, one of the richest men in the world, contends that there are no financial gurus. He is given credit for the following statement (KNPR, Feb. 2001): "Do not use financial advisors for your investing. They take from 1 to 3% of your money and whether they are right or wrong, you still must pay them. Instead, learn all you can about investing and do it yourself." These two messages reinforce that it is up to you to learn all you can regarding money management and reducing your spending so you will have more money to invest.

Because the market indexes do go up and down and there are no gurus, you need to be your own advisor. Professional advisors sometimes hit and sometimes miss, but no one can tell you which way the indexes will go on a regular basis. People can make predictions, but there are no guarantees. Who could have predicted a 23% decline in the market in 1987? Who could have foreseen that the last five recessions would be followed by market recoveries that were each better and higher than before? Fluctuations are normal, and all investors need to accept them, as uncomfortable as that may be. This is regarded as risk. How risk tolerant are you regarding your investing? I will discuss risk in the next section.

Using the lines below, write a paragraph summarizing three or more things you learned from this section.

_____

_____

_____

_____

_____

Recognizing Investment Risk: What Is My Risk Tolerance?

OK, you make a plan. Your plan requires that you make monthly investments. Most investments involve risk. The higher the interest rate of return, usually, the more the risk. **KEY:** *High returns equal high risks.* How much risk can you handle? No one will pay you high interest rates for investing in a sure thing. In most cases, the higher the interest rate offered to investors, the more there is a risk of losing some, or all, of the money invested. Diversification of assets, which we will focus on later, is the best protection against risk.

No one wants to take unnecessary risks, but there is always some degree of risk in making an investment. But thinking only about investment risk can expose you to another, less obvious risk: losing out to inflation.

Again, there is no way to invest without incurring some level of risk. Admit it: You dream of a safe haven for your money. You want a place where your money will grow and be protected from risk. Such a place doesn't exist. Risk is inherent in *all* investments. The key is to balance risk with potential reward.

How much and what type of risk should you assume? One way to answer this question is to consider the amount of time that you have available for your investments to grow. Money plus time at a certain percentage of return equals a certain dollar growth. The amount of time you have to recoup any potential losses is a good measure of how much risk it is wise to accept.

Bonds and stocks do carry risk. **KEY:** *There is no investment without risk.* Inflation is also a risk—one that many people don't consider. If you don't consider inflationary risks, you could find your retirement savings falling short of your expectations. Are your investments staying ahead of inflation?

Your investments will fail to keep pace with inflation if the interest rate is lower than the rate of inflation. Isn't this a horrible thought? You are actually gambling that your money will increase at a rate greater than inflation. If your money does not keep up with inflation, you lose purchasing power, which can dramatically reduce the likelihood of your achieving your financial goals. For example, if the inflation rate is 3% and your investments return 5%, you're really only making a 2% profit on your money. A 2% return is not the stuff of which retirement dreams are made. Even a moderate inflation rate can have a dangerous effect on an investment portfolio over time.

The best defense against the risk is a *diversified portfolio.* Investing in a combination of stocks, bonds, and cash funds gives you some protection against risk. This is because different types of investments typically don't react in the same way to changing economic conditions. One may perform well when another doesn't, reducing the overall impact on your portfolio. Although there are no truly safe havens, don't be penny wise and pound foolish, either. Put some money in higher-risk investments, such as stocks. Generally speaking, you should invest in a combination of investments. You can afford to be more aggressive when you're younger and have more time to recoup potential losses, but if market gyrations keep you awake at night, limit your exposure to stocks—no matter what your age.

Things to Remember About Risk

Investment risk and inflation risk aren't an either/or proposition. Most investments involve more of one type of risk and less of the other. To reduce one type of risk, you generally have to increase the other. Here are some things to remember about risk:

- Generally, the higher the risk, the higher the potential for reward, but the reverse is also true.
- Short-term investments and bonds are generally less risky than long-term investments, but historically they have offered lower returns than stocks over the long term.
- Stocks are among the most risky investments in the short term, but they offer the potential for the highest return in the long term. History suggests that the longer you invest in stocks, the higher your potential return becomes. Remember that past performance is no guarantee of future results.
- The shorter the time period you have for investing, the more conservative (less risky) your investments should be.

However, some 60-year-olds still invest as if they were 20, 30, or 40, and some 20-year-olds invest as if they were 60. The bottom line: If you can handle the risk, go for it. If you can't handle it, select more conservative funds and investments. Don't let anyone convince you against your better judgment that "you can make lots of money if you do this or that." If you feel uncomfortable about an investment, trust yourself and don't do it.

Minimizing Risk Through Diversification

The bottom line is, you must diversify. Some people like individual stocks, whereas others prefer investing in stock mutual funds (SMFs). There are no sure bets, but over the last 10 years it has been found that, regardless of downturns and upturns, 80% of SMF funds have paid annual returns of 17%. Check for yourself if you doubt this. And it gets better. For the past 20 years, 80% of stock mutual funds have paid annual returns of 15%. In fact, if you go back almost 70 years, you will find that 80% of stock mutual funds have paid returns in the neighborhood of 13%. This is the reason many investors hold on to mutual funds—domestic or international. Using stock mutual funds, you can still diversify by buying equity funds—growth, stock, sector, international/world, or global—and fixed-income funds—bonds (corporate, government, or city) and money markets. (Each of these terms will be explained in the Terminology section.) Be aware that you cannot control for risk, but by studying investment options, you can tailor your investments to match your risk tolerance.

Using the lines below, write a paragraph summarizing three or more things you learned from this section.

_____

_____

_____

_____

_____

Becoming a Wiser Investor

Don't let the market scare you. The Dow and the other indexes can be jumpy one week and relaxed the next. That is the way Wall Street operates. Investors love it when indexes go up. It means that they are reaping financial rewards. In fact, in the 1990s many became millionaires. However, just as the indexes can go up, they can also go down, and so can investors' fortunes. Many of these same millionaires could possibly experience financial difficulty or ruin in the future. **KEY:** *There are no financial gurus.*

Who would have predicted the Nasdaq would rise to exceed 5,000 or that the Dow would exceed 11,000? In turn, who would ever have expected the Nasdaq to drop more than 60% and the Dow to drop 25%, in less than a year? This is the excitement of being an investor, because when you invest for the long haul, you end up riding these waves.

You can read the advice of all the financial "experts," and there are many—Lynch, Price, Driehaus, Gabelli, Sloate, Sharpe, Ryback, Sherman,

Miller, Friess, Murray, and Shaw, to name a few. Yet when the market goes down, these money managers, financial advisors, and financial educators, like the rest of the American public, remain worried about their financial futures. Learn from the past and the unpredictable nature of the market. Stay the course. Be cautious, but not reckless. **KEY:** *There is no quick fix or easy cure when the market goes down.* The pattern has always been that it goes down and then comes up again. In the last couple of decades, the market has bounced back nine times and it will do so again.

Since World War II, despite nine recessions and many other economic setbacks, corporate earnings have increased by 63 times and the stock market has risen by 71 times. Corporate profits per share have grown over 9% annually, despite the down years. Nine percent may not sound like a lot, but consider what it means when profits mathematically double every 8 years, quadruple every 16, are up 16 times every 32 years, and rise 64 times every 48 years. This is just a simple regurgitation of the Rule of 72.

The Rule of 72 and Problems to Solve

Here is a simple calculation to help you understand the power of time, amount invested, and compound interest. Take any amount of money, say $1,000. Put it into a fund paying 9% interest annually. To learn how quickly this investment will double, divide 9 into 72; the answer is 8. This means that in 8 years your $1,000 investment, in a fund paying 9%, will be worth $2,000. By using this Rule of 72 you can determine how many years it will take for your investment to double.

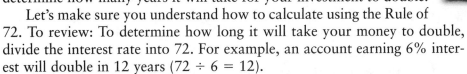

Let's make sure you understand how to calculate using the Rule of 72. To review: To determine how long it will take your money to double, divide the interest rate into 72. For example, an account earning 6% interest will double in 12 years ($72 \div 6 = 12$).

What does this tell you? For one thing, it tells you that such a return would not be a good investment if it is just barely keeping up with inflation. However, it would be safer than a 9% or 12% investment return (because, as I explained earlier, more aggressive investments carry higher risk). But the questions remain: How soon do you need to have your money double, and how much risk can you handle? It is great to find a fund that may return 24% a year, but if it goes up or down 50 points every day, you might get an ulcer worrying about it. As you've heard me say before, you need to judge the level of risk you can handle.

Here is another way to figure out the return you will need on your investment. If your invested money doubles every 12 years and according to financial advisors, it must double a minimum of 6 times in your working lifetime, then you would have to work for 72 years ($12 \times 6 = 72$). Because on average most people expect to work for 36 years, you need a fund or other investment that pays an annual return of 12%. This will allow your investment to double 6 times in a working lifetime of 36 years.

Let's have some fun. Solve the following Rule of 72 problems. See how easy it is to do the calculations.

PROBLEM 1.

You find a savings fund paying 3% interest. If you invest $1,000 in this fund, how long will it take for this fund to reach $2,000? _____ . How old (answer + your age) will you be then? _____ .

PROBLEM 2.

You find a fund paying 4% interest. This one is a CD (certificate of deposit). You invest your $1,000 in this fund. How long will it take for this fund to reach $2,000? _____ . How old (answer + your age) will you be then? _____ .

PROBLEM 3.

This problem has five parts:

[A] You find a fund that has the potential of earning 8% or more annually. This investment is known as a stock mutual fund (SMF). If you invest your $1,000 in this fund and its average annual return is 8%, how long will it take for this fund to reach $2,000? _____ . How old will you be then? _____ .

[B] If the SMF averages an annual return of 9%, how long will it take for this fund to reach $2,000? _____ . How old will you be? _____ .

[C] If this same SMF pays an average annual return of 10%, how long will it take for this fund to reach $2,000? _____ . How old will you be? _____ .

[D] If this SMF pays an annual average return of 11%, how long will it take for you to see your $1,000 double to $2,000? _____ . How old will you be? _____ .

[E] Suppose this SMF performs very well and averages an annual return of 12% on your $1,000 investment. How long will it take for your money to double to $2,000? _____ . How old will you be? _____ .

More fun ahead! Complete the following chart. You will need to use the answers from Problem 3.

NAME   DATE

TREASURE CHEST

Complete each section in each column below. Your answers in Y will give you
a rough indication of how long you must work to achieve your financial goal.
Your answers in Z will indicate the minimum age you will be at that time.

U	V	W	X	Y	Z
PROBLEM #3	INTEREST RATE	YEARS NEEDED TO DOUBLE INVESTMENT	DOUBLED TIME MULTIPLIED BY 6	MINIMUM NUMBER OF YEARS TO EXPECT TO WORK	ADD EACH Y ANSWER TO YOUR CURRENT AGE TO GET THE AGE THAT YOU CAN EXPECT TO RETIRE
A	8%		× 6 =		
B	9%		× 6 =		
C	10%		× 6 =		
D	11%		× 6 =		
E	12%		× 6 =		

Caution: This looks simple, but please be aware that with each 1-point increase in percentage return on
your investment you incur a greater degree of risk. This means that what goes up can also go down.
There are no guarantees. You need to be comfortable with your own risk level. Don't let the hope for *big*
dollars guide your decisions.

Using the lines below, write a paragraph summarizing what you learned from doing this exercise.

_____

_____

_____

_____

_____

_____

_____

What the Rule of 72 Means to You

The Rule of 72 has its strengths, but it also has its weaknesses. Overall, the rule tends to be remarkably accurate for interest rates of 18% and lower, but for rates above this amount, there is some inaccuracy. If you want to check the rationale underlying the rule, go to www.moneychimp.com/features/rule72.htm. *Caution:* This website is not for the math-phobic person.

What does the Rule of 72 mean to you as an investor? Had you put $1,000 away 32 years ago and not touched the money but let it grow and compound at an average interest rate of 9%, your $1,000 would be worth approximately $164,036 today. Had you invested two, three, or four times that amount, your portfolio would be worth between $328,072 and $656,144. A little money does grow a considerable amount over time, depending upon the interest rate.

The amount of money earned over each eight-year period is shown in Exhibit 2.3. Notice that your money doubles every eight years at a 9% annual interest rate. Considering that you invested only $32,000 over those 32 years and your return was $164,000, then your gain was $132,036.

Are you aware that $1,000 per year equals $2.74 per day? Or $19.23 per week? Or $84 per month (using a 13 month calendar)? How often have you wasted $3 a day, $21 a week, or $84 a month? It takes only a small investment with regular contributions and an average rate of return left to grow for 30 or more years, to yield a fairly large nest egg.

Using the lines below, write a paragraph summarizing three or more things you learned from this section.

exercise

_____

_____

_____

_____

EXHIBIT 2.3	$1,000 INVESTED FOR 32 YEARS AT A RETURN OF 8% ANNUALLY.			
YEARLY INVESTMENT	**AFTER 1ST 8 YEARS**	**AFTER 2ND 8 YEARS**	**AFTER 3RD 8 YEARS**	**AFTER 4TH 8 YEARS**
$1,000	$11,028	$33,003	$76,789	$164,036

Go to www.sovereignbank.com/calculate/ to locate the calculator used to compute these figures. When you get to this website—*Savings Calculators*—bring up the link in the file titled "How much will my savings be worth?"

Learn from the Past

Don't become alarmed when the market and the indexes drop. There have been recessions, but realize that there have been balancing events, as well. In the last 50 years, there have been many periods of economic prosperity and many periods of uncertainty. Despite 9 recessions, 3 wars, 2 presidents shot (one died and one survived), 1 presidential resignation, 1 presidential impeachment trial, and the Cuban missile crisis, stocks have been good investments throughout.

Moreover, since World War II, recessions have been less severe (the severity of job loss has trended downward during recessions from 1948–1991), are shorter (average duration is 1 year and average recovery is 4–8 years), and have not gotten out of control. Historically, the United States has had a perfect record when it comes to rebounding from difficult times. With 9 recessions, there have been 9 recoveries.

The thing to remember when you invest is that you invest for the long term. The market and your money need time to adjust to change and to grow. Despite painful periods when investment values go down, you will be pleasantly surprised at how your money grows over the long haul. Avoid speculating and invest for the long haul.

KEY: *Dollar-cost-averaging is a means of having some control over your contributions by investing regularly.* Dollar-cost-averaging is a process wherein you invest regularly—during both good and bad times. You buy when low, but you also buy when high. You ride the ups and downs of the market by buying the funds over the year. The cost of your investment is averaged over time—thus the term *dollar-cost-averaging.* Many people contribute to their retirement fund by having their employer take money out of each payroll check. Or you can do it yourself by establishing a monthly plan and sending in your investment on an every two– or every four–week basis. In either case, you are a wise investor because you make contributions on a regular basis.

Economic and financial history reveal that over the long haul, 80% of stock mutual funds have shown growth. This has been true for the past 10, 20, and 65 years. The bottom line is that you, the investor, must believe in the strength of resolve, hard work, and innovation and then take a long-term view and believe in the U. S. economic system. With a positive attitude toward the investment system, you should be pleased with the results.

Using the lines below, write a paragraph summarizing three or more things you learned from this section.

exercise

_____

_____

_____

_____

Making Wiser Choices: It Is Up to You

You need to decide to use your money wisely. Do not, for instance, gamble that you will have enough money for your retirement by gaming at one of the casino tables. Instead—to echo a main theme of this book—make a conscious choice to learn all you can about money and money management.

Do not pay anyone to make your financial decisions for you. It would be a waste of money. Remember Warren Buffett's quote. Instead, learn how to do it yourself. It will definitely pay you dividends.

There is no real secret to having and making money. It makes no difference whether you are rich or poor, old or young, male or female. You can have wealth beyond your wildest imagination.

You will see how easy it is to make a budget and a plan and to stick to them, to create a goal and to stick to that. Be focused and determined; work hard at learning all you can, and be willing to accept the rewards. To do all this, you need to study, study, study. Without study there is no learning.

TREASURE CHEST

E   X   E   R   C   I   S   E

Using the lines below, write a short summary of what you learned as a result of reading this chapter. Make it a point to list at least *three* KEYS in your writing. Indicate clearly how you expect to use these KEYS to guide your financial life.

_____

_____

_____

_____

_____

_____

_____

_____

_____

_____

_____

_____

_____

_____

_____

_____

_____

_____

_____

_____

_____

3

THE BEST PATH TO
THE BEST INVESTMENTS

STUDY! STUDY! STUDY!

Learning and Understanding the
Language of Money and Finance

Like every area of specialization, the field of money and investing has it own
language. It is important to get a handle on the terminology and jargon
related to the field. Quickly, terms that were new to you will become old
hat. You will come to understand and speak the language like a professional investor and money manager.

Have you heard someone you know say: "I just got a bonus check from
my job—what should I do with it? I thought about spending it, but then I
think that may be wasteful. I should begin to think about my retirement and
investing it, but I hear so many strange terms, and it is all confusing to me.
Should I put my money in a bank savings account or start a Christmas Club
account? What is a CD or a money market certificate? Do you know anything about stock, mutual funds, or that thing called an IRA?"

The world of finance, with its jargon and acronyms, can be intimidat-
ing to the new investor. Don't let the fact that there's a lot to learn keep you
from joining a group of savvy, knowledgeable people. It is exciting to learn
about money. Each investor has had to deal with this language. With a little practice, you too will learn the terminology. Don't let money managers
discourage you from learning about investing and becoming financially
independent. You can and should be your own money manager, so now is
the time to learn the language.

Bond and Stock Mutual Funds

Mutual funds offer convenient options for beginning investors. Investing in stocks and bonds directly is difficult due to the large amount of up-front money required and the sophistication of timing the market and making the right choices. In addition, investing directly in stocks and bonds usually requires a broker, and the commissions you pay the broker may eat up your profits. For these reasons, investing in individual stocks and bonds is generally unwise for beginners. Of course, as your assets grow, it may become more appropriate for you to consider such an investment. Most young or new investors, however, would do best to stick with mutual funds.

What is a mutual fund?   A mutual fund is a pool of stocks, bonds, or money-market securities (e.g., short-term debt obligations such as treasury bills) that the fund's manager acquired to earn investors the best possible return on their investment. You invest in a mutual fund by purchasing shares. This makes you a part owner—along with thousands of others—of the pool of securities that the fund manager has assembled. Your holding entitles you to a proportionate share of the fund's earnings.

Why invest in mutual funds?   There are a number of excellent reasons to invest in mutual funds. First, mutual funds have full-time professional managers selecting securities and monitoring them 24 hours a day. Second, a mutual fund gives you the kind of diversification—often through hundreds of different stock and bond issues—that most of us couldn't afford as independent investors. Should one or two of the stocks drop, the rest of the fund's holdings will cushion the loss and protect your overall investment. Third, investing in mutual funds requires only a modest amount of money.

Most mutual funds require a minimum initial investment of $1,000; some have minimums of $250 and $500; and others have no minimum at all. It is possible, then, to invest $25 per week ($100 per month) in funds with the potential of earning more than 10 to 12% a year. You could eventually select to invest in several different mutual funds—say two stocks, two bonds, and one money market—and thereby diversify as broadly as a multimillionaire can.

Another advantage of mutual funds is that the fund manager usually has a staff that calculates, usually daily, the risk involved with any mutual fund purchase. You can actually purchase mutual funds known for being low, moderate, or high risk. The more "volatile" a fund is, the more risk there is for the purchaser. With a little study, you can determine which mutual funds match your risk tolerance. Usually a young person is a more likely candidate to purchase funds with high volatility than someone who is older and nearer to retirement. However, there are many older and retired investors whose high tolerance for risk leads them to take the risks a 20-year-old might. It is a personal thing.

How much risk is there in a mutual fund? Unlike banks, mutual funds have no insurance; instead, custodial banks hold their securities. If the fund company collapses or one of its managers runs off to Brazil, generally your holdings will be safe. However, this does not mean that your money is protected against loss.

As stated earlier, when you invest, you expose yourself to some risk. Perhaps you remember that fateful period from December 2000 to March 2001, when the market dropped a whopping 35%. Or maybe you remember October 16, 1987, when the average stock fell almost 21%.

Those times were very scary for big and small investors. Market downturns can actually be good for investors, however. If you remember, the market of 1987 rebounded and experienced fantastic growth for its investors until December 2000. The key to investing wisely is not to panic when your mutual funds begin to fall. **KEY:** *Hang in there; your funds will usually turn around.* (Note the word "usually." There are no guarantees.) The downturn of the early 2000s is still making itself felt, and the upturn may take another five or six years before the consequences can be determined. If the past is any indication, however, a turnaround is not too far away.

How does one select a mutual fund? This can be a dilemma for new investors. There are more than 3,000 funds from which to choose; this may be overwhelming. Initially, you may want to choose a broad-based fund, to spread your risk among many securities. Later, as you build your assets, you can sample funds that are more aggressive (see Exhibit A.6 in the appendix).

Mutual fund earnings are seen as three separate parts:

- dividends (interest) on securities that the fund owns
- profits on securities the fund sells
- appreciation in value of fund shares

Funds that emphasize income (dividends or interest) usually pay monthly returns. Funds that aim for growth over time pay either annually or semi-annually.

Picking the fund or funds to invest in depends on your personality and your tolerance for risk and uncertainty. If you think that you will sweat buckets and stay up nights if your fund loses 10 percent of its value in 10 weeks, then perhaps a volatile fund is not the best choice for you. (Some people are still holding funds the value of which has dropped more than 40 percent. The rationale is that they were good choices when first bought, and they are still good choices. These highly volatile fund choices may still be good choices. If—note the word "if"—the investor is correct, their value could even double or triple in the next five to six years.) On the other hand, if you choose a fund so conservative that the share price hardly varies, you may as well stay with CDs (certificates of deposit). Consider the following KEY as a rule of thumb. **KEY:** *The riskier the investment, the higher the potential payoff.*

KEY: *The nearer you are to needing the money, the more conservative your investment should be.* Conversely, if you are saving for something 20 years into the future, you could take greater risk.

If you lose some of your money, you will still have years to recover it and earn more. For instance, from December 2000 through the third quarter of 2001, many people have continued to hold on to the investments they had before the downturn. Their belief is that the turnaround is a short time (maybe 5 to 10 years) away. **KEY:** *In the world of investments, 5, 10, 20, or 30 years and more are considered short time spans for money to regroup and bounce back.*

Using the lines below, write a paragraph summarizing three or more things you learned from this section.

_____

_____

_____

_____

_____

_____

Important Investment Terminology

This section presents a compilation of definitions for some of the common terms investors use. I hope you will make it a habit to refer to this section to get a better understanding of the material you encounter in this book. The terms are not difficult to learn, and after using each of them a few times, you will probably assimilate them into your vocabulary. With a little practice you will find that using "moneyspeak" is fun.

Actively managed funds: A mutual fund in which the fund manager is allowed to use his or her discretion to buy, sell, or hold investments in the portfolio. Most investors choose mutual funds because of the manager's active involvement in their management.

Aggressive growth fund: A type of mutual fund in which the manager concentrates on "hot" stocks, in the belief that they will go even higher. This type of fund is suitable for investors who can hold shares for 5 or more years and who have a high tolerance for risk. These funds have the potential to turn the best long-term performance, but they are riskier than other funds.

Asset allocation: The division of money among various types of investments, such as stocks, bonds, and short-term investments.

Balanced fund: Sometimes called a "hybrid" fund, a balanced fund is a type of mutual fund that invests in a combination of stocks and bonds. This type of fund is appropriate for someone seeking an investment that is more conservative than pure equity funds. Traditionally, balanced funds invest approximately 60% of their assets in stocks and 40% in bonds. However, many balanced funds have of late increased their exposure to stocks. These funds aim to provide steady income from dividends and interest. They are appropriate for people who can hold shares for 5 or more years but are not comfortable with the more aggressive funds, such as growth funds.

Blue chips: A nickname for large, established companies.

Bonds: Bonds are essentially loans. Bonds are issued by government agencies, such as the U. S. Treasury, and by corporations, to raise money. A bond certificate is like an IOU: It shows the amount loaned (principal), the rate of interest to be paid on the loan, and the date that the principal will be paid back (maturity date).

Bond fund: A type of mutual fund in which the manager invests in bonds. For investors who are retired or approaching retirement, this type of fund is safer than stocks or stock mutual funds. These funds are designed for people who need a steady cash stream in the present. Bond funds are not without their dangers, however. Bond funds often invest in ventures with very high yields and associated high risk; for example, bond funds may be invested in the bonds of municipalities or companies with low credit ratings. This places investors' money at considerable risk. Too, a bond fund can boost its yield by holding bonds that will mature in 10 years or more. This could prove to be problematic for a conservative investor, because when interest rates rise, bond prices fall. Therefore, a longer maturity date means the bond must live up to its potential for a longer period of time. The most secure bond funds are those that invest in bonds of credit-worthy institutions and that mature within 2 to 5 years.

Certificate of deposit (CD): A guaranteed savings certificate issued by banks. In general, CDs pay low rates of interest, although there have been cases where longer-term CDs have returned 16% annually. CDs currently pay under 5% annually. CDs are appropriate for the older investor who wishes to protect her principal investment. CDs just barely keep ahead of inflation.

Diversification: The concept of investing money in different kinds of vehicles, to moderate investment risk—i.e., not putting all your eggs in one basket. A diversified portfolio can shield an investor from large losses because if some securities falter, others may perform well. Diversification neither ensures a profit nor guarantees against loss.

Diversified fund: A type of mutual fund in which the manager invests in a wide array of types of stocks—often more than 100 securities—to reduce risk.

Dividends: Payments distributed by corporations to shareholders. Although historically companies have used dividends to share profits and entice shareholders to buy their stock, fewer firms pay out dividends today, choosing instead to use the capital to buy back shares, reinvest in the company, or invest in other companies. Some dividend-oriented mutual funds have loosened their investment rules to adapt to these trends.

Dollar-cost-averaging: A strategy whereby investments are made regularly—often monthly—during good and bad times (both when the market is high, and when it is low). Using this strategy, an investor can ride the ups and downs of the market by buying the funds over the years. The average of what was paid into the investment is the "dollar-cost-average."

Dow Jones Industrial Average (Dow or DJIA): The most widely used indicator of how the United States' leading industrial companies are performing. The average is calculated using a formula based on the stock prices of 30 of these companies. They are chosen from the sectors of the economy most representative of the country's economic condition. The 30 stocks in the Dow Jones Industrial Average are: AT&T Corp., AlliedSignal Inc., Aluminum Co. of America, American Express Co., Boeing Co., Caterpillar Inc., Citigroup Inc., Coca-Cola Co., Walt Disney Co., DuPont Co., Eastman Kodak Co., Exxon Corp., General Electric Co., General Motors Corp., Hewlett-Packard Co., Home Depot Inc., Intel Corp., International Business Machines Corp., International Paper Co., Johnson & Johnson, McDonald's Corp., Merck & Co., Microsoft Corp., Minnesota Mining & Manufacturing Co., J.P. Morgan & Co., Philip Morris Cos., Procter & Gamble Co., SBC Communications Inc., United Technologies Corp., and Wal-Mart Stores Inc.

Equity-income fund: A conservative type of stock mutual fund in which the manager seeks dividend income as well as capital appreciation. These funds provide steady income from dividends and interest. They are appropriate for investors who can hold their investment for 5 years or more but are not comfortable with the more aggressive funds.

Flexible income fund: A type of mutual fund that combines stocks and bonds to give good payouts, even when the market drops. These funds are designed for a person who needs a steady cash stream in the present. Flexible income funds are not without their dangers, however. Flexible income funds often invest in ventures with very high yields, but the bond offered may be invested in the bonds of municipalities or companies with low credit ratings. This places investors' money at considerable risk. Too, a flexible income fund can boost its yield by holding mostly bonds that will mature in 10 years or more. This could prove to be problematic for a conservative investor, because when interest rates rise, bond prices fall. Therefore, a longer maturity date means the bond must live up to its potential for a longer period of time. The most secure flexible income funds are those that invest in bonds of credit-worthy institutions and that mature within 2 to 5 years.

Global (international) fund: A type of mutual fund in which the manager focuses on foreign investments. This is a type of diversified investing; if some of an investor's assets are in global funds, this will help safeguard her total portfolio. "Only buying American" is unheard of in modern investing. Global funds can fall into the categories of bond, stock, or mutual fund, depending on the kinds of securities in them. Despite the Euro, one danger posed by global funds is currency fluctuation. Because the funds' investments are denominated in foreign currencies, the value of the holdings depends on the strength of the U.S. dollar relative to the foreign currencies. When the dollar is strong, the return is reduced because it costs more to redeem shares for U.S. dollars. When the dollar is weak, however, the return is increased because it costs less to redeem shares for U.S. dollars.

Growth fund: A type of stock mutual fund in which the manager seeks out shares of companies with rapidly expanding earnings and/or revenue. Stocks are bought when the share price has been steady but is expected to move up shortly.

Growth and income fund: A type of diversified stock mutual fund in which the manager seeks both growth and dividend income. Stocks are bought with the belief that high dividends are near. These funds aim to provide steady income from dividends and interest. They are appropriate for investors who can hold their investment for 5 years or more but are not comfortable with the more aggressive funds.

Index fund: A passively managed fund that tracks an existing stock market benchmark, such as the Standard & Poor's 500 index of blue-chip stocks.

International fund: A type of mutual fund in which the manager hunts for stock abroad. It usually happens that when the U.S. economy goes down, the international economy rises. There is no guarantee that this will happen, but it is advantageous to have some international funds in one's portfolio mix. (See also Global funds.)

Market index: An indicator of financial performance. Indexes tend to specialize in one sector of the market. The *Dow* includes 30 stocks of blue-chip companies (estimated sales in 2000 ranging from $14.3 billion to $194.5 billion). The *S&P 500* casts a somewhat broader net, tracking the performance of 500 stocks; again, it tends to include only stocks of big companies (the smallest company in the index earns $188 million in revenues). The *Nasdaq* includes some 5,100 stocks, tilted heavily toward the technology sector. According to Barron's (November 15, 1999), large technology stocks accounted for approximately 71% of the Nasdaq's 50% gain during the first eleven months of 1999. Most other indexes include only a tiny fraction of technology companies. Indexes have other characteristics, as well. For example, the Dow is a price-weighted index, which means that changes in the value of high-priced stocks have the greatest impact on its performance. Indexes are useful in reporting on the gains and losses of a narrow market sector, for instance, the household products industry or the beverage industry.

Nasdaq Composite Index: An unmanaged index of about 5,000 over-the-counter stock prices. The Nasdaq does not assume the reinvestment of dividends. The acronym stands for National Association of Securities Dealers Automated Quotations system.

New-economy fund: Fund that invests in a cross-section of technology, telecommunications, and other stocks that stand to benefit from the developing technology- and information-driven economy.

Rule of 72: A calculation that enables one to determine how long it will take money to double, in value. The rule is that you divide the interest rate into 72. For example, an account earning 6% interest will double in twelve years ($72 \div 6 = 12$).

Sector fund: A type of mutual fund in which the manager invests in a single sector of the economy, such as financial services, health care, precious metals, technology, or utilities. This type of fund is suitable for investors who can hold shares for 5 or more years and who have a high tolerance for risk. These funds have the potential to turn the best long-term performance, but they are riskier than other funds.

Short fund: A mutual fund that makes bets that the stock market (or at least certain stocks) will fall in value—and then tries to profit from those losses. Some funds do this by "shorting" a stock. Short selling is the reverse of the more typical buy-low, sell-high approach to investing. Here, you borrow a security from a brokerage and then sell it on the open market. When the price of the stock tumbles, you then "repurchase" the security, hopefully at much lower prices. You then return the security to the brokerage, pocketing the difference between the higher price at which you borrowed the shares and the lower price at which you repurchased them. Short funds are appropriate only for knowledgeable investors. Selling short is more gambling than investing.

Short-term investment: Investments of typically under 10 years. Short-term investments help bring stability to a portfolio. They provide current income and seek to preserve the principal of the investment. They also tend to provide the lowest returns over the long term. Examples of these investments include certificates of deposit (CDs), Treasury notes, and money-market instruments.

Standard & Poor's 500 Index (S&P 500): An unmanaged market capitalization–weighted index of common stocks. The S&P 500 is a registered service mark of The McGraw-Hill Companies, Inc. and has been licensed for use by Fidelity Distributors Corporation and its affiliates.

Stock: A partial ownership in a company. How much you own depends on how many shares of stock you have. Holders of common stock are the last to be paid any profits from the company but are likely to profit most from the company's growth. Owners of preferred stock are paid a fixed dividend before owners of common stock are paid, but the amount of the dividend usually doesn't grow if the company grows.

Treasury note: A guaranteed note issued by the U.S. Treasury. In general, Treasury notes pay low rates of interest—currently between 5 and 6% annually. These are appropriate for the older investor who wishes to protect her principal investment. Treasury notes just barely keep ahead of inflation.

Using the lines below, write a paragraph summarizing three or more things you learned from this section.

exercise

_____

_____

_____

_____

_____

Fund Plans/Programs: A Gift from Your Government

The U.S. government has created certain retirement savings plans that may be considered "gifts" by those that use them. These programs are most commonly called *TSA*'s, or *tax sheltered annuities*. TSA programs include Keogh, Roth IRA, traditional IRA, and 401 and 403 plans. There are yet many more TSA plans, but these are the ones most commonly used by the average investor. Each of these plans pays dividends, and when correctly managed (by *you*) can provide income throughout your retirement years. They usually provide tax savings on all or a portion of your investment. In the following pages, I will give basic information about these TSA plans; I would encourage you to enroll in a money management class at your local community college or university to learn about them in greater depth.

IRAs: Two Types

Traditional IRA (individual retirement account). Individual retirement accounts offer both tax deductions and long-term tax incentives for saving. The rules concerning IRAs were changed a few years ago to prevent some taxpayers from claiming a deduction for their contributions. However, even though this retirement fund may not be for everyone because of this restriction, more than 75% of the working population is eligible to participate in this program.

An IRA contribution cannot exceed the taxpayer's earned income. This includes self-employment income as well as wages. Since 2002 each member in a family can make contributions up to the allowed amount. (See Exhibit 3.1 for new allowable contributions.)

In the case of a non-working spouse the allowable amount increased from $250 (prior to 2002) to a maximum contribution of $2,000. A separate account is required to be maintained for each spouse. Of course, each employed spouse may contribute up to the maximum allowable amount to his or her own account. The money goes in untaxed and grows tax deferred. In addition, the new Act lifts restrictions on rollovers between various types of retirement accounts and assets. Exhibit 3.1 illustrates the limits on contributions and the increases scheduled to take effect each year.

The major advantage of a traditional IRA is that it allows you to put pre-taxed dollars from your paycheck into an investment fund, lowering your current tax, and to earn interest on this investment without paying immediately any tax on the interest.

Be aware, however, that taxes *will* be due on the money you take out when you are eligible to make withdrawals from your IRA (at 59½ years of age). Before this time, the money is not actually available to you. (*Note:* The previous statement is not entirely accurate: If you need your money before you reach the stated age, you can make withdrawals, but you will pay taxes and penalties for early withdrawal.) **KEY:** *Put into an IRA only money that you will not need immediately.*

Roth IRA. The Roth IRA does not allow for you to take pre-tax dollars and place them in investment funds. Instead, you must use after-tax dollars

| EXHIBIT 3.1 | IRA CONTRIBUTION AND WORKPLACE SAVINGS. |

CONTRIBUTION & LIMITATIONS*		
	IRAs		401(k) & 403(b)
YEAR	Under 50 years of age	Additional catch-up amount for those over 50 years of age	
2001	$2,000	0	$10,500
2002	$3,000	$500	$11,000
2003	$3,000	$500	$12,000
2004	$3,000	$500	$13,000
2005	$4,000	$500	$14,000
2006	$4,000	$1,000	$15,000
2007	$4,000	$1,000	
2008	$5,000	$1,000	

* The limits set for the IRA accounts will be adjusted for inflation for 2009 and above, and the limits for 401 & 403 accounts will also be adjusted for inflation beginning after 2007.

Source: CCH Business Owner's ToolKit (2002). Retrieved 6/25/02 from www.toolkit.cch.com/text/p08_4820.asp 401(k) & 403(b) and *Mutual Funds Magazine* online (February 2002). Retrieved 6/25/02 from www.mutual-funds.com/mfmag/stories/2002/february/retirement/new_rules_2.html.

to make these investments. However, the Roth does allow this money to grow untaxed. Therefore, over the years, you do not pay any tax on the interest being earned on your investment. More good news: With the traditional IRA, you pay as you withdraw money from your investments, but with the Roth IRA, you pay no tax on withdrawn money.

This can prove to be a significant advantage during your retirement years. Let's set up an example. Let's say that you have a traditional IRA and you withdraw $5,000 each month to live on. You have limited deductions, and you find yourself in the 28% tax bracket. Thus, you will receive only $3,600 from your $5,000 retirement fund. However, if your money is in a Roth IRA, there is no tax on your investment. Therefore, your monthly check will be the full $5,000.

Look at Exhibit 3.2. It calculates contributions of $88 and $166 made each month into an IRA with 10% and 12% rates of return. Note that the money will grow over 40 years to more than $500,000 at $88 per month and to almost $1,000,000 at $166 per month at 10% return. The results are even better at a 12% return. If this were a Roth IRA, the money would be untaxed. There are contribution limitations: an income maximum of $110,000 for a single person and $160,000 for a couple. Approximately 3% of working people are excluded from Roth IRAs.

Keogh Plan

A Keogh plan—also known as an HR-10 plan—is a tax-deferred retirement savings plan for people who are self-employed. It is much like an IRA. The main difference between a Keogh and an IRA is the contribution limit. Although exact contribution limits depend on the type of Keogh plan, in general a self-employed individual may contribute up to a maximum of $30,000 yearly and deduct that amount from his taxable income.

The following information was derived from material provided by T. Rowe Price regarding their small company plans. There are three types of Keogh plans. All types limit the maximum contribution to $30,000 per year, but additional constraints may be imposed depending on the type of plan.

1. *Profit Sharing Keogh:* Annual contributions are limited to 15% of compensation but can be as low as 0% for any year.

2. *Money Purchase Keogh:* Annual contributions are limited to 25% of compensation but can be as low as 1%. Once the contribution percentage has been set, however, it cannot be changed for the life of the plan.

3. *Paired Keogh:* Combines profit sharing and money purchase plans. Annual contributions are limited to 25% but can be as low as 3%. The portion contributed to the money purchase part is fixed for the

EXHIBIT 3.2	$1,000 AND $2,000 INVESTED FOR 40 YEARS IN AN IRA.

AGE	NO. OF YEARS	$1,000 INVESTED YEARLY IN IRA (APPROX. $88/MO) AT 10% ANNUALLY	$2,000 INVESTED YEARLY IN IRA (APPROX. $166/MO) AT 10% ANNUALLY	$1,000 INVESTED YEARLY IN IRA (APPROX. $88/MO) AT 12% ANNUALLY	$2,000 INVESTED YEARLY IN IRA (APPROX. $166/MO) AT 12% ANNUALLY
25	1	1,100	2,200	1,120	2,240
26	2	1,210	2,420	2,254	4,508
27	3	3,431	6,862	3,525	7,050
28	4	4,774	9,548	4,948	9,896
29	5	6,252	12,504	6,542	13,084
30	6	7,877	15,754	8,327	16,654
31	7	9,664	19,328	10,326	20,652
32	8	11,631	23,262	12,565	25,130
33	9	13,794	27,588	15,073	30,146
34	10	16,173	32,346	17,882	35,764
35	11	18,791	37,582	21,027	42,054
36	12	21,670	43,340	24,551	48,266
37	13	24,837	49,674	28,497	56,994
38	14	28,320	56,640	32,916	65,832
39	15	32,152	64,304	37,866	75,732
40	16	36,367	62,734	43,410	86,820
41	17	41,004	82,008	49,619	99,238
42	18	46,105	92,210	56,574	113,148
43	19	51,715	103,430	64,362	128,724
44	20	57,887	115,774	73,086	146,172
45	21	64,675	129,350	82,856	165,712
46	22	72,143	144,286	93,799	187,598
47	23	80,357	160,714	106,055	212,110
48	24	89,393	178,786	119,782	270,310
49	25	99,332	198,664	152,374	304,748
54	30	166,088	332,176	274,888	549,776
59	35	301,937	693,874	490,799	981,598
64	40	492,378	984,756	871,309	1,742,617

life of the plan, but the portion contributed to the profit sharing part (still subject to the 15% limit) can change every year.

Like an IRA, the Keogh offers the individual a chance for her savings to grow free of taxes. Taxes are not paid until the individual begins withdrawing funds from the plan. Participants in Keogh plans are subject to the same restrictions on distribution as IRAs—namely, distributions cannot be made without a penalty before age 59½, and they must begin before age 70½.

Setting up a Keogh plan is more complicated than establishing an IRA. As a result, you would do well to seek out a competent brokerage house that can help you execute the proper paperwork.

More Choices: Saving Plans

In the late 1990s, self-directed retirement accounts, including 401(k)s and IRAs, topped the $1 trillion mark. What's the best way for you to make your next $1,000,000,000,000? 401(k), IRA, or both?

401(k). Since its introduction, the 401(k) has been the most popular type of retirement savings plan. The primary benefits to employees are listed below.

- *Immediate tax savings.* Because you make contributions to the plan *before* taxes are deducted from your income, you pay less in current taxes.

- *Long-term tax savings.* Your investment earnings grow and compound tax-free until you withdraw them from the plan. And your tax bracket may be lower after you've retired than it is while you are working, further reducing your tax bill.

- *Company match.* If your employer is one of the many who contribute to their employees' 401(k) accounts based on the employees' own contributions, this greatly enhances your savings rate. Employers often allow employees to contribute as much as 10%, 15%, or 20% of their pay into the 401(k) plan. At the same time, federal regulations limit the amount each employee can put in the plan yearly (see Exhibit 3.1 for the specific amount).

The employer match is actually free money—a bonus for which you pay no taxes. A match is an employer's contribution to the employee's 401(k) plan based on the amount the employee contributes for himself. Typically, this match is based on a percentage of the employee's contribution, up to some maximum contribution amount. For example, a company formula may stipulate that the employer will match 50% of an employee's contributions up to a maximum of 6% of her salary. If an employee contributes 10% of her salary to the plan, the employer would contribute an additional 5% of that employee's salary. If the employee stepped up her contributions to 12% of her salary, the employer would kick in the maximum 6% match.

Here's a more detailed example that shows how powerfully this affects your retirement savings. Two 30-year-old employees, each making $33,334 per year, participate in their employers' 401(k) plans. They both contribute 12% of their pay to these plans. One employer has a matching policy, and the other does not. Let's assume the match is the amount given in the previous example: 50% of the employee's contributions, up to a maximum of 6% of the employee's salary. At the end of the year, the employee without an employer match would have contributed $4,000 (rounded off to the nearest $100.) to his plan. The employee with the match would also have contributed $4,000, but in addition, her employer would have contributed another $2,000, for a total contribution of $6,000. At age 60, assuming an annual investment return of 8%, the account would grow to $453,132 for the unmatched employee and $679,999 for the employee who got the match. The extra $226,566 is free money. It is most beneficial to contribute enough to get the maximum contribution from your employer.

Roth IRA. Roth IRAs provide some benefits that are similar to those of a 401(k) plan, but they do differ, as described below.

- *Long-term tax savings.* Unlike the situation with a 401(k) or traditional IRA, contributions to a Roth IRA are made on an *after tax* basis, so there are no immediate tax savings. However, both principal and interest from a Roth can be withdrawn tax-free after 5 years, with very few restrictions. This can add up to sizable long-term tax savings.

- *Freedom of choice.* With a 401(k), unless you are an owner-employee or happen to be the benefits manager at your company, your investment choices are limited to what your employer chooses to offer to you. With an IRA (either traditional or Roth), you choose your retirement savings investments.

Choices. Until the introduction of the Roth IRA in 1997, most financial planners suggested maximizing your 401(k) contributions first. If you still had money to invest for retirement, they would then recommend an IRA. Traditional IRAs don't allow fully deductible contributions if you are eligible for an employer-sponsored plan like a 401(k), and therefore end up being after-tax. This disadvantage is somewhat offset by the fact that the investment earnings grow tax-free until retirement.

Today, retirement professionals suggest contributing an amount to your 401(k) that maximizes the company match (since that amounts to free money from the company) and then putting your next $2,000 per year into a Roth. Next, they suggest depositing any additional amounts back into your 401(k) up to the maximum allowed. To put this in list form:

1. 401(k) up to the maximum company match (pre-tax)
2. Roth IRA for the next $2,000 in savings (after-tax)
3. 401(k) up to the plan or legal limits (pre-tax, after-tax)

403(b) plan. This plan is similar to a 401(k) plan—it is a retirement savings plan that is funded by employee contributions and (often) provides matching contributions from the employer.

403(b) plans are not "qualified plans" under the tax code, but generally are higher-cost "tax-sheltered annuity arrangements" that *can be offered only by public school systems and other tax-exempt organizations.* 403(b) plans invest in annuities or mutual funds only. The traditional way to fund a 403(b) is with employee contributions through a prearranged salary reduction. The amount deducted from the employee's salary is then contributed by the employer to the 403(b) account. The advantages of a 403(b) account are similar to those for a 401(k) plan:

- There are tax incentives.
- There are investment advantages.
- You pay no current taxes on earnings.

Withdrawals are possible, but as with a 401(k), this is discouraged. This is because your tax-deferred contributions and tax-sheltered earnings on the contributions are intended for use in your retirement years. Therefore, the IRS allows withdrawals from your 403(b) account only for one of the following reasons: you have reached age 59½; you have separated from service or employment with the organization, or you have become totally and permanently disabled.

As long as your money stays in a 403(b) plan, it will grow untaxed, similar to a 401(k) plan. However, all distributions will be taxed as ordinary income. If the distribution is considered an "eligible rollover distribution," it is subject to an automatic 20% withholding unless it is transferred by a direct rollover to either an IRA or another 403(b) plan. In addition, any distribution taken before age 59½ may be assessed a 10% penalty tax because the IRS considers it a premature withdrawal of retirement benefits. Lastly, as with a 401(k) plan, distributions from a 403(b) must begin by age 70½ to avoid tax penalties.

There are many choices to make regarding your economic future. This is why a college or university class on investments and money management is so helpful.

KEY: *The key to getting the most out of your investment programs is choosing a portfolio with a mix of funds, so that it can weather bad times and prosper in good ones.*

Using the lines below, write a paragraph summarizing three or more things you learned from this section.

_____

_____

_____

401(k) caution alert. I need to include a cautionary note for all 401(k) investors (which does not seem to be necessary for investors in 403(b) plans). You need to watch for warning signs that your 401(k) plan may be in trouble or being abused (see Exhibit 3.3). If you have observed any of these signs, make it a point first to check with the Financial Office at your place of employment. Someone there may be able to provide a perfectly good explanation for the problems. If there isn't a good explanation, however, you may be wise to seek legal representation. Although abuses are rare, there are cases on record of employers who have abused their 401(k) plans by using employee contributions for company purposes or by holding on to the money too long.

EXHIBIT 3.3   TEN WARNING SIGNS THAT YOUR 401(K) PLAN MAY BE IN TROUBLE.
1. Your 401(k) or individual account statement is consistently late or comes at irregular intervals.
2. Your account balance does not appear to be accurate.
3. Your employer failed to transmit your contribution to the plan on a timely basis.
4. A significant drop in account balance cannot be explained by normal market ups and downs.
5. 401(k) or individual account statement shows your contribution from your paycheck was not made.
6. Investments listed on your statement are not what you authorized.
7. Former employees are having trouble getting their benefits paid on time or in the correct amounts.
8. Unusual transactions, such as a loan to the employer, a corporate officer, or one of the plan trustees, appear on your statement.
9. There have been frequent and unexplained changes in investment managers or consultants.
10. Your employer has recently experienced severe financial difficulty.

TREASURE CHEST

Using the lines below, write a short summary of what you learned as a result of reading this chapter so far. Much material was covered regarding financial terminology and the various types of retirement savings programs. Identify at least *three* ideas to guide your financial life.

_____

_____

_____

_____

_____

_____

_____

_____

_____

_____

_____

_____

_____

_____

_____

_____

_____

_____

_____

_____

_____

_____

A College Education: The Best Investment You Can Make

The best financial investment that you can make, at any age, is a college education, even though there are stories about people making "big" money without a degree. Many people dream of becoming a millionaire—by either earning or inheriting money. Having rich parents is indeed a good way to become rich; approximately 10% of the "super rich" did acquire their wealth that way. What may surprise you is that *keeping* wealth takes considerable work and study. Even people who have inherited their wealth can gain much from a college or university degree.

Besides working hard, financially successful people usually get a solid education before achieving their eventual financial success. For example, producer and director Steven Spielberg has a B.A. in English from California State University. Warren Buffett, second-richest man in the world, founder at age 25 of Buffett Partnership and Chairman of the Board and Chief Executive Officer of Berkshire Hathaway, Inc., studied at The Wharton School of the University of Pennsylvania, earned a B.A. from the University of Nebraska, and received an M.S. in Economics from Columbia University. Noted award winning television news personality, Barbara Walters is a graduate of Sarah Lawrence College. *Dateline NBC's* Jane Pauley earned her B.A. in political science from Indiana University. Secretary of State Colin Powell, the former chair of the Joint Chiefs of Staff, graduated from City College of New York. Peter Lynch of Fidelity fame has a B.S. degree from Boston College and an M.B.A. from The Wharton School of the University of Pennsylvania.

I could also list several non–college educated individuals who took the risk to start a business without a college education, relying only on their determination and drive. Bill Gates (the richest man in the world) is a college dropout. Wayne Huizenga (billionaire and founder of Blockbuster Video) also dropped out of college, and self-made billionaire Kurt Kerkorian (primary stock owner of MGM/UA) left high school in his junior year. Ted Turner, dismissed from his university, later returned to graduate. However, whatever you do, please don't drop out of school just because some people were able to become rich without a college education. **KEY:** *Education is one of the most worthwhile investments you can make.*

The nondegreed financial mavens mastered the skills needed to succeed in the world of business: creativity, ingenuity, perseverance, focus, determination, and hard work. None of them left school to avoid work or to party. Instead, they dropped out to start a business and to devote all their energy to their dream. Even today, with millions and billions of dollars at their disposal, they continue to work, create, and dream. These people are still doing what they dreamed of doing.

They provide a good lesson for all of us: Create a dream and learn what you need to know to make the dream a reality. They were willing to put everything into making their dream succeed. With study, determination, and focus, you too can make your dream of wealth a reality.

Randy Fitzgerald, in the *Reader's Digest* article "You Can Make a Million" (July 1996, p. 26), quotes Thomas J. Stanley, the head of the Affluent Market Institute, Atlanta, regarding wealth: "Wealth is more often the result of hard work, perseverance, and most of all, self-discipline."

In reality, hard work may not be enough to achieve financial independence, wealth, and security, however. In spite of the fact that there are notable examples of people who became financially successful without completing college or even with less than a high school education, the general consensus is that the greatest investment one can make is to earn at least an associate's degree, and if possible a bachelor's degree. In fact, "Spare Change" (*Family Money,* September/October 2000) reported that it did not matter if one attended a select college or the neighborhood one. It takes discipline and tenacity to complete a college degree, no matter where you study. The more education you have today, the greater is your likelihood of achieving financial success. Furthermore, although it may sound paradoxical, if you apply for employment at a company headed by a non–college educated executive, the hiring officer will in all probability ask you to provide evidence of having earned an undergraduate or graduate degree.

Therefore, the best investment is more than attending college—it is earning a college degree. If you haven't already, you must begin now to take your education seriously. Do not skip classes, it is like throwing money away. Instead, attend each class and take advantage of your books and your professors. You paid for these resources. Use them!

If you want to earn a comfortable retirement, you have a big leg up if you complete at a minimum a two-year degree. A high school education is the absolute minimum. If you are to earn a middle-range income or higher, it is mandatory that you complete high school. As the world becomes more technologically oriented, higher levels of education will be a huge advantage. **KEY:** *Stay in school.*

Using the lines below, write a paragraph summarizing three or more things you learned from this section.

exercise

_____

_____

_____

_____

_____

The Facts About Staying in School

According to the Department of Commerce, Bureau of the Census (1999), two-year college graduates earn $700,000 more in their working lifetime than high school graduates do. This amounts to more than a $20,000 difference per year. Is this difference a substantial one to you? Could you use some of that money for monthly contributions to an investment fund? Study Exhibit 3.4.

Exhibit 3.4 combines the 1999 median yearly annual income for all male and female workers 25 years old and over by level of education. The last two columns project the minimum possible income for this same group into the year 2234, using a 3% inflation figure. Not included in these figures is any consideration of promotions, raises, and merit increases for any group listed. The only comparison is by educational level.

This exhibit clearly illustrates the value of staying in school and earning a degree. A person 25 years old or more with a high school diploma or equivalent (that is, a G.E.D.) will have a median annual income of $28,398. A person that does not earn a high school degree can expect an income 28%

EXHIBIT 3.4	COMBINED MEDIAN ANNUAL INCOME OF YEAR-ROUND, FULL-TIME WORKERS (ALL GROUPS) 25 YEARS OLD AND OVER, BY EDUCATIONAL LEVEL FOR 1999 PROJECTED TO 2234 (USING A 3% INFLATION FIGURE AND NO COLA).

EDUCATIONAL ATTAINMENT	**CENSUS BUREAU CALCULATIONS** 1999 YEARLY MEDIAN INCOME		**PROJECTED TO 2234** YEARLY MEDIAN INCOME	
	MONTHLY	**YEARLY**	**MONTHLY**	**YEARLY**
9th–12th grade (no diploma)	$ 1,703	$ 20,437	$ 3,383	$ 57,506
High school graduate or G.E.D.	$ 2,367	$ 28,398	$ 6,659	$ 79,908
Some college, no degree	$ 2,777	$ 33,328	$ 7,815	$ 93,780
Associate's degree	$ 2,986	$ 35,827	$ 8,401	$100,812
Bachelor's degree	$ 3,836	$ 46,032	$10,794	$129,528
Master's degree	$ 4,738	$ 56,861	$13,333	$159,999
Doctor's degree	$ 6,274	$ 75,282	$17,653	$211,833
Professional degree	$ 7,374	$ 88,491	$20,730	$249,001

Data source: U. S. Department of Commerce, Bureau of the Census, Table 8: *Income in 1999 by Educational Attainment for People Working at 25 Years of Age and Over: March 2000.* December 19, 2000. Online: www.census.gov/population/socdemo/education/p20-536/tab08.txt/ (October 9, 2001). (Not included in the calculations is median income standard error of measurement.)

less than that of a high school graduate. That high school degree is worth almost $8,000 more per year to the recipient. Persons who stay in school and earn an associate's degree can expect to earn a yearly income of $35,827. Those who stay in college or university for two more years and earn a bachelor's degree see their median income increase to $46,032.

In 2234, 35 years later than 1999, with a minimum inflationary increase of only 3%, the high school graduate can expect $79,908, whereas the two-year college degree holder can expect to earn $100,812 (a $21,000 difference). With a bachelor's degree, the median income rises to $129,528 (almost a $30,000 difference). The bottom line: *Stay in school*. Get your education and your degree.

Today, the median cost of living for a family of four is in the neighborhood of $32,500. Based on Exhibit 3.4, people with some college or an associate's degree earn incomes at that level. The average worker will work for between 30 and 40 years. Using 35 years as an average working life, in 35 years a middle-class family will need to have an estimated medium income of $91,450. A worker with an associate's degree can expect his income will grow to $99,892, accounting for only 3% inflation.

KEY: *College is an investment in your future.*

Using the figures cited in Exhibit 3.4, then, the difference in salary between a person with a high school diploma and someone with an associate's or bachelor's degree can be as much as $20,000 to $30,000 per year over a working lifetime. A four-year college or university graduate can expect to earn $1,200,000 more than a high school graduate earns during a 35-year working lifetime. This difference of $30,000 to $50,000 each year can amount to millions when even 60% is invested in a retirement fund. Again, *stay in school*.

People with college degrees who have the discipline to put away $9,000 or $15,000 each year will have no difficulty saving for their retirement years. This would mean investing $750 per month (for $9,000) or $1,250 per month (for $15,000). Actually, many people and families do invest such amounts for retirement. See Exhibit 3.5 for the surprising reality of how much could be saved over time by investing at this level.

Most people find it difficult to put away such large lump sums each year, however. Therefore, instead of considering investing $750 or $1,250 each month, let us consider lesser amounts, $88 or $166. Would you be surprised to realize that this small amount of money can equal $1,000,000 in as little as 35 years? Exhibit 3.6 shows the calculations of $88 and $166 invested each month for 35 years at set interest rates of 8 to 12%. Were you surprised that you can accumulate this much money by putting away $22 or $44 each week? Many individuals and families waste this much money each week on items that are non-necessities.

EXHIBIT 3.5	INVESTMENT GROWTH AS A RESULT OF CONTRIBUTING $9,000 AND $15,000 EACH YEAR AT A SET RATE OF INTEREST.

ANNUAL PERCENT INTEREST/ RATE OF RETURN	CONTRIBUTIONS FOR 5 YEARS		CONTRIBUTIONS FOR 10 YEARS		CONTRIBUTIONS FOR 20 YEARS		CONTRIBUTIONS FOR 35 YEARS	
	$9,000/ year	$15,000/ year	$9,000/ year	$15,000/ year	$9,000/ year	$15,000/ year	$9,000/ year	$15,000/ year
8	52,799	87,999	130,379	217,298	411,857	686,429	1,550,851	2,584,752
9	53,862	89,770	136,736	227,893	460,441	767,401	1,941,396	3,235,661
10	54,945	91,576	143,436	239,061	515,474	859,124	2,439,219	4,065,365
11	56,050	93,417	150,498	250,830	577,825	963,042	3,074,305	5,123,843
12	57,175	95,292	157,938	263,231	648,471	1,080,786	3,884,971	6,474,952

EXHIBIT 3.6	INVESTMENT GROWTH OF MONTHLY CONTRIBUTIONS OF $88 AND $166 EACH MONTH FOR 35 YEARS AT A VARIETY OF SET RATES OF INTEREST.

ANNUAL PERCENT INTEREST/RATE OF RETURN	CONTRIBUTIONS FOR 35 YEARS	
	$88 PER MONTH	$166 PER MONTH
8	201,861	380,784
9	258,877	488,336
10	334,104	630,241
11	433,690	818,097
12	565,924	1,067,539

Redo your Brief Monthly Financial Statement Worksheet (Exhibit 3.7), and then complete the following exercise. What non-necessities can you eliminate from the expense side? Can you find money to invest in your retirement? When you subtract expenses from income, how much do you have left? How much of this are you willing to use for investing?

Understanding how much money you waste, and then minimizing that waste, increases your potential for achieving wealth more than you might have thought possible. You can amass $500,000, or even $1,000,000 within your working lifetime. It is easy, if you plan now.

BRIEF MONTHLY FINANCIAL STATEMENT WORKSHEET.	**EXHIBIT 3.7**

AS OF (Date)

ASSETS/INCOME	$ AMOUNT	LIABILITIES/EXPENSES	$ AMOUNT
Monthly Taxable Income		Rent/Mortgage	
Cash in Pocket		Utilities — Gas/Electric	
Savings — All Sources/Locations		Phone(s)	
Money in Bank Account(s)		Internet and Cable TV	
Other Assets:		Grocery/Food/Cleaning Stuff	
		Credit Cards	
		Loans	
		Insurances	
		Snacks	
		Junk Food	
		Eating Out	
		Gas for Car	
		Unplanned Activities	
TOTAL ASSETS		TOTAL EXPENSES/LIABILITIES	
		TOTAL ASSETS	
		LESS MONTHLY LIABILITIES	
		AMOUNT LEFT FOR INVESTING	

1. What can you cut from your current expenses that would give you money for investing?

_____

_____

2. Where else can you find money you can use for investing?

_____

_____

3. Would you use the money that you find to invest?   ❏ Yes   ❏ No

4. When you start wasting less money, will you use the saved money for investing?   ❏ Yes   ❏ No   (Of course, this choice is for you to make.)

Using the lines below, list two or three ideas or keys that you learned from this section.

_____

_____

_____

_____

Sources of Financial Aid: Attending College Free or Pretty Close to It

Are you aware that for many college students, the cost of a college education is *free?* As you learned in the last section, in today's marketplace it is important that you earn at least an associate's, and preferably a bachelor's, degree. Therefore, study the types of assistance that can be available to you for college or university study. There are scholarships, grants, loans, and work-study opportunities.

City, State, and Federal Awards

What programs are there for students who do not have honor grades or special talents? Have no fear; there is assistance for most students. Local, state, and federal money is available for all levels of higher education. Did you know that the amount of money available is more than $10 billion each year? That's one followed by *nine* zeros! What is amazing is that almost half this money goes unused, because students do not apply for it.

In this section, I will describe the most popular financial aid funds and programs. Others also exist. You can contact your local high school transfer office or the admissions office of your local community college, college, or university to learn more about financial aid. You can also access either of the following URLs: www.ed.gov/prog_info/SFA/StudentGuide/ or www.ed.gov/. They are the two largest government websites about student aid.

If you have no computer access, your high school does not have the information you need, or you are not near a college or university, dial the

Federal Student Aid Information Center Hotline at 1-(800) 4-FED-AID (1-800-433-3243). Loan information is available through Educaid, which has student loan specialists available at 1-(800) EDUCAID (1-800-338-2243). Do not delay—call these numbers today and learn about the funds available for your use. To receive consideration for these funds, you need to apply. So call!

Many students are surprised that they may only be a postage stamp or a call away from receiving $500, $5,000, or more in city, state, and federal money for each year they attend college—usually full-time. There is also money for students who need to attend part-time, however. Wouldn't money from your city, state, or federal government make it a little easier to attend college? Many financial aid awards could reduce your college costs by 30 to 60%. Isn't it worth the effort and time to investigate what is available to you?

Scholarships and Grants

The most common financial aid programs are scholarships and grants. These are aid awards. They don't have to be repaid. If you have honor grades, you may be able to get a scholarship to attend two-year or four-year colleges and universities. Athletic talent, musical ability, or other skills that make you a particularly attractive candidate to some institutions may also put you in line for a scholarship.

On the other hand, you may qualify to receive a grant. Although you are not required to repay a grant, some grant programs require that you perform a service in exchange for the award. The recipient of a band grant, for example, may be required to devote time to rehearsals and playing his instrument at college football games. This is a small price to pay for the opportunity to attend college. Two of the more common grant programs are: PELL (www.ed.gov/prog_info/SFA/StudentGuide/2000-1/pell.html/) and FSEOG (Federal Supplemental Educational Opportunity Grant, at www.ed.gov/prog_info/SFA/StudentGuide/2000-1/fseog.html/).

Pell Grant. The Pell is a federally administered grant. It is not repayable. Federal Pell grant awards go only to undergraduates who have not earned a bachelor's or a professional degree (such as law, dentistry, or pharmacology). For many students, Pell grants provide much of the foundation money in their total financial aid packages. A recipient of a Pell grant can have other aid awarded to them based on need. Pell grant money can be awarded for less than full-time attendance, although in that case the award is reduced. For more information on the amount of a Pell award, an individual needs to contact the institution he or she plans to attend. The information is also found at the URL address given in the previous paragraph.

Pell Grant Eligibility: Financial aid eligibility is determined by the Student Aid Report (SAR), which each applicant must fill out. The U. S. Department of Education uses a standard formula, established by Congress, to evaluate the information provided in the SAR. The formula produces an expected family contribution (EFC) number. Subtract the EFC from the cost of attendance (COA), and the result is the student's financial need (COA – EFC = financial need).

For additional information regarding federal Pell grants, call 1-800-433-3243 or write to Federal Student Aid Information, P.O. Box 84, Washington, DC 20044.

FSEOG. How do FSEOG and Pell grant programs differ? The U. S. Department of Education guarantees that each participating school will receive enough money to pay Pell grants to its eligible students. However, there is no guarantee that every eligible student can receive a FSEOG, because those funds are based on availability. FSEOG funds are intended for undergraduates with exceptional financial need, that is, students with the lowest expected family contributions (EFCs). All students who receive FSEOG awards also receive Pell grants. Neither of the grants needs to be paid back. An FSEOG award can vary from as little as $100 to as much as $4,000 per year.

For more information regarding the Federal Supplemental Education Opportunity Grant, you can call or write the Federal Student Aid Information office (phone number and address given previously) or go to the website (also given earlier).

Loans

A loan is a specified sum of borrowed money that must be repaid after you complete your degree. To qualify as financial aid, loans must carry an interest rate lower than prevailing commercial rates. They must also offer favorable repayment provisions.

Repayment schedules vary with the lender. Some lenders require you to start repaying if you drop to part-time; others allow a part-time semester as long as during the year you attend one semester full-time. Some give you as much as one year from graduation to begin repaying the loan. For example, the Stafford Loan Program does not require borrowers to start paying interest on the loan nor do they have to retire any of the principal until nine months after completing their studies. No one rule fits all lenders, so you need to know the specifics of your particular loan.

Work-Study

Work-study is the third-most-popular financial aid program, after scholarships/grants and loans. The financial aid office at the college or university arranges the work opportunities. Employment may be on-campus or off-campus. Many colleges require that work-study recipients be full-time students. (The exact credit-hour minimum for full-time attendance status varies from college to college; it's usually 12 semester hours or 15 term hours.) The financial aid office also regulates the number of hours a student may work each week. Under normal circumstances, students work 15 hours per week; under special circumstances, however, arrangements for 20-hour workweeks are possible. Work-study programs encourage community-service work and work related to a student's course of study. For more information about financial aid, contact the financial aid office at the college or university you plan to attend.

A Final Financial Aid Note: Be Time Conscious

Arranging for financial aid in time for the beginning of a new semester takes planning. **KEY:** *You cannot leave applying for financial aid until the last minute.* Application forms need to be completed. Then the forms must be mailed to the Federal Office on Student Assistance in accordance with specific date guidelines. These steps take time. Failure to turn in your financial-aid application on time will result in a delay in receiving your money. Students often have to wait an entire semester if they miss the deadline for turning in their paperwork. Make sure that you turn in your paperwork with time to spare.

The financial aid office gets the information it needs about you from your application. Some of the information that you turn in needs to be notarized (another time-consuming step). Also, your income tax reports—your parents' and/or yours—will be needed, to verify the income that you claim.

If you are to use the abundant financial aid money that is available to you, you cannot wait until the last minute to get it. Procrastination means paying a greater portion of college costs than you need to.

Using the lines below, write a paragraph summarizing three or more things you learned from this section.

exercise

_____

_____

_____

_____

_____

TREASURE CHEST

EXERCISE

Using the lines below, write a short summary of what you learned as a result of reading this chapter. Make it a point to list at least *three* **KEYS** in your writing. Indicate clearly how you expect to use these KEYS to guide your financial life.

_____

_____

_____

_____

_____

_____

_____

_____

_____

_____

_____

_____

_____

_____

_____

_____

_____

_____

_____

_____

_____

_____

4

DISCOVERING HIDDEN MONEY

Patching Up the Hole in Your Pocket

Do you remember the section in Chapter 2 on making wise choices? Being able to find the money to invest has to do with the choices you make.

People frequently say they cannot save for retirement because of pressing demands on their finances. Bills, children's needs, and unexpected expenses make it difficult to save for retirement. How many students say they have no money for anything, yet as they speak, they are eating a dinner roll, drinking a cup of coffee, and smoking a cigarette. Or they complain about being short of funds and come to class with a Big Gulp and a donut. "Cognitive dissonance" is the term psychologists use to describe this type of behavior—it is a method that allows you to lie to yourself. To find the money to invest, you need to stop lying to yourself. Are you willing to do this?   ❏ Yes   ❏ No   I hope your answer to this question is yes!

KEY: *Successful saving requires you to be honest with yourself.* It is easy to save, but to do so, you will have to change the little day-to-day expenses that add up in the long run.

Imagine what would happen if you put some of the money that you spend on snack food, dinner, movies, or impulse buying toward saving for retirement. It might not seem like much at first, but these simple tradeoffs do add up over time, as Exhibit 4.1 demonstrates. At the Fidelity website, http://personal300.fidelity.com/toolbox/spendorsave/spendsaveinput.html, there is a wonderful Spend and Save calculator for your use. Little changes equal big savings.

Exhibit 4.1 is hypothetical, showing examples of savings in a tax-deferred account and based on a 9% annual rate of return compounded at

EXHIBIT 4.1	POSSIBLE AREAS OF SAVINGS, CALCULATED FOR A 30-YEAR PERIOD.

POSSIBILITIES FOR CUTTING BACK	ESTIMATED SAVINGS	ESTIMATED GROWTH
Doing "take-out" vs. dining out once a month	$45/month	$ 83,001
Spending less on dry cleaning	$7.50/week	$ 60,099
Reducing new clothes purchases	$400/year	$ 59,430
Buying cappuccino every other day instead of daily	$7/week	$ 56,092
Exercising at home vs. gym membership	$300/year	$ 44,572
Less frequent manicures	$15/month	$ 27,667
Snacking	$90/month	$166,002
Renting a video vs. seeing a movie once a month	$11/month	$ 20,289

the same rate as contributions over a 30-year period. I do not mean to indicate that any investment product will perform as indicated in this example. The calculations are done using today's dollars. For an example, let's take snacking. It can add up to $90 a month. If you choose to put this snacking money into an IRA account—either traditional or Roth—and allow it to grow tax-free, at the end of the 30-year period at 8% annual interest, it would have grown to $134,132 (see Exhibit 4.2). And this is just one spending habit.

EXHIBIT 4.2	THE RESULTS OF SAVING $90 PER MONTH IN AN IRA AT VARIOUS ANNUAL RATES OF RETURN.

RATE OF RETURN AT ANNUAL PERCENT	$ AMOUNT CONTRIBUTED TO MONTHLY	IRA TRADITIONAL OR ROTH		
		10 YEARS	20 YEARS	30 YEARS
8	90	$ 16,465	$ 53,012	$ 134,132
9	90	$ 17,416	$ 60,110	$ 164,767
10	90	$ 18,436	$ 68,343	$ 203,444
12	90	$ 20,703	$ 89,033	$ 314,547

In the chart below, identify the things for which you believe you spend unnecessarily. Think of what it costs you daily, weekly, and monthly. If you are to do this correctly, you will need to be honest with yourself.

UNNECESSARY SPENDING ITEM	DAILY EXPENSE	WEEKLY EXPENSE	MONTHLY EXPENSE
Eating out			
Snacking			
Movies			
Video rentals			
Cell/telephone			
Morning coffee with donut or other pastry			
Buying clothes on a whim			
ATM fees			
Cigarettes			

What did you discover from doing the exercise on unnecessary spending?

_____

_____

_____

Are there areas where you will now admit that you are wasting money? ❏ Yes ❏ No

If you did not spend this money or spent less, how much would you be willing to put into an investment fund for your retirement? Be realistic and honest.

_____

_____

_____

exercise

Using the lines below, write a paragraph summarizing three or more things you learned from this section.

_____

_____

_____

_____

_____

_____

Know Your Financial Situation

Before committing yourself to any major expense, know your net take-home pay. (Net income is what remains of a paycheck after taxes and other mandatory deductions.) Then estimate how much income is likely to be available to you. This is another way of ensuring you make wise choices. The general recommendation is that you defer any purchase—excluding large purchases such as a home, a car, or a college education—until you have the cash.

Having a successful financial plan is based on knowing your financial situation. Know your assets (what you own), your current debts (what you owe), your current needs, and your future expenses. Take a minute to figure out your financial situation. This will help you budget more accurately.

Complete the Assets vs. Debts Balance Sheet that follows. Is your net worth positive or negative? If your net worth is positive, that is terrific! You can begin now to plan to set aside a small portion of your money for long-term investment.

If your net worth is negative, then there is work to do. First, you need to examine where you are spending your money. Second, you need to develop a financial plan with the goal of getting your net worth to the plus side. This will require you to develop and keep a financial budget.

Don't let the word "budget" scare you. There are many myths about budgets, but the bottom line is that a budget is a plan. People who use a budget actually find that they end up with more money than they did without one.

ASSETS VS. DEBTS BALANCE SHEET

AS OF (Date)

ASSETS		LIABILITIES	
Real Estate		Mortgage(s)	
Personal Property		Taxes	
Autos		Operating Expenses	
ACCOUNTS RECEIVABLE		ACCOUNTS PAYABLE	
Cash			
Savings		Insurance Premiums	
Checking			
CDs		Charge Accounts	
Stocks			
Mutual Funds		Loans (payments due others)	
Bonds			
Government Bonds		Installments	
Pension			
Annuity		Credit Cards	
Profit Sharing			
Cash-Value Life Insurance		Other Liabilities	
Loans (payments receivable)			
Other Assets			
TOTAL ASSETS		TOTAL LIABILITIES	
		TOTAL Assets	
		LESS Total Liabilities	
		NET WORTH	

What is your debt status? Do you know your debt-to-income ratio? Complete the Current Debt Status chart, which was adapted from *The Money Book of Personal Finance* (Eisenberg, 1996), to calculate it.

CURRENT DEBT STATUS

Loans and charge accounts:
(Do not list first mortgages or credit cards paid in full each month.)

Last Month's Payments

_____	$ _____
_____	$ _____
_____	$ _____
_____	$ _____
_____	$ _____
_____	$ _____
_____	$ _____
_____	$ _____
_____	$ _____
_____	$ _____

1. Last month's total payments $ _____
2. Monthly after-tax income $ _____
3. Your debt-to-income ratio $ _____

   Divide line 1 by line 2. This is the percentage of your take-home pay that goes to pay your non-mortgage debt.

4. See the table below to determine if you have too much debt.

	Your Debt-to-Income Ratio			
Your Age	**0–10%**	**10–15%**	**15–20%**	**20%+**
Under 35	A	A	B	C
35–55 (one wage-earner in household)	A	B	C	C
35–55 (two wage-earners in household)	A	A	B	C
Over 55	A	B	C	C

Code Explanation:

A = You are doing fine.
B = Watch it.
C = You are in trouble.

What did you find out about your debt? Are you in the A, B, or C range? Generally, an acceptable level of debt is a 36% or less debt-to-income ratio.

To use an Internet calculator to determine your debt-to-income ratio, go to www.culand.com/debt.html/ and use Credit Union Land, Inc.'s free calculator. If you fall below the 36% level, that's great. If you are above this percentage, however, you need to determine what you can do to correct this situation. How can you take better control of your cash flow? There are so many money wasters and enticers out there. These enticers can rob you blind and prevent you from attaining financial wealth today and in the future.

Using the lines below, write a paragraph summarizing three or more things you learned from this section.

_____

_____

_____

_____

_____

The Enticers: Watch Out for Financial Pitfalls

It's so basic: Most people's financial problems stem from spending more money than they bring in. As stated in several other sections, the best way to solve this is to spend less. This, of course, is more easily said than done. Take note of those things you buy that you think you need but really don't. You could use the money you spend on unnecessary items for savings, education, and investing instead.

Gambling

Gambling is not a need, but it certainly can be an enticer! You must decide whether you prefer to take chances with your money or to make careful choices about your financial resources. You can come to Las Vegas, where I live, and take a chance on winning a million dollars or more. Realize, however, that of the more than 36 million people visiting Nevada each year and possibly gaming at the many casinos, only six (6) are likely to win that million dollars. Money spent this way is *not* a good investment. The odds of winning are not in your favor.

To give you a little more insight into gambling, remember that each new hotel that opens is paid for not by the rewards of winning but by the money lost by those who *don't* win. Many of these billion-dollar hotel/casinos pay off their bank notes in 24 to 36 months. That's a lot of money taken from those who sought to make it big instead of investing!

Snacking

Snacking is one of the most dangerous enticers. A rough observation shows students spending $20 or more a week on unnecessary food purchases. How many bags of chips, bottles of soda, candy bars, and cookies do you buy each week? You may suffer from the "munchies," but take responsibility for what those "munchies" are costing you.

You don't have to eliminate junk food, but you must make a plan regarding the purchasing of these products. For instance, instead of buying your snacks from a vending machine, go to the grocery store once a week and buy them. You'll save 75% through using that strategy alone. This just goes to show that you do not have to be rich or take huge steps to save money for retirement. **KEY:** *Be cautious and diligent in managing your budget.*

Some of you are probably thinking, "Where can I find places where money I am saving will earn 8%, 9%, 10%, and higher annually?" In other chapters of this book, you learn about funds that pay interest rates this high, and you are introduced to several individual retirement programs. The government's intent with these programs is to provide to its working citizenry financial opportunities to help them save and invest for retirement. Failure to take advantage of these opportunities means you lose out on obtaining the wealth that awaits each of you. **KEY:** *Successfully saving money requires you to be open to change.* Are you willing to make changes? You must avoid allowing old behaviors to guide you when it comes to effective money management.

A TRUE CONFESSION FROM A FOOD JUNKIE

I have to admit that in the past I, too, was guilty of wasteful spending—to satisfy my craving for snacks. For instance, I used to drink three Cokes a day. Then I cut it down to one Coke a day, and I found a place that only charged me 25 cents for a 20 oz. bottle. However, when I was buying three Cokes a day, I was spending about $3.00 per day—unnecessarily.

If I bought only one bag of chips or one package of cookies per day (and it was often more than that), this would add another $1.25. Roughly, $4.00 a day, or $22.50 a week, equals $90 a month. If I had taken that $90 and invested it in a fund paying 10% or more interest, at the end of 40 years, I would have more than $500,000 set aside. I would not only be richer, but also thinner and healthier by not eating that junk! Surprise! I cut out the junk food, and I watch my food intake. I have more money to invest, and I have lost 42 pounds.

To have money for tomorrow requires that you plan, save, shop sensibly, and invest wisely today. **KEY:** *Most of your investment capital will come from money you already have.* Are you surprised?

Do not get trapped into thinking you need a second or third income to set money aside for future financial independence. It is much easier than that. Most people do not realize they have the necessary capital. It depends upon how wisely you spend it and invest it.

Grocery Shopping

Grocery stores can be sources of bad decisions about spending as well. **KEY:** *Never go to the grocery store hungry.* A hungry shopper usually buys more food than she really needs, and often the purchases are not healthy or necessary ones. So, go shopping only after you have eaten. **KEY:** *Buy only items that are on your shopping list.* Impulse buying can become very expensive.

The next activity will take some legwork to complete, but it will be worth it. Comparison shopping can result in savings of $100 or more per month. What could you do with an extra $100 each month? Would you believe that $100 a month placed in an investment fund for 40 years at a 10% annual return rate will grow to $632,408? Watching your grocery shopping can lead to big savings and money for investing.

Directions for the Comparative Shopper Grocery Store Exercise

This exercise is good for both men and women. If you have a significant other and/or children, it would be great if you do it together. You must make a commitment to do this exercise for seven consecutive days. You cannot miss a day during the selected week.

The Comparative Shopper Worksheet has two sides. Before completing the worksheet, make a copy of it. Then, in the event that you find you have made a mistake, you can redo it on your copies. Be sure to copy both sides of the worksheet.

The estimated time for completing this exercise is approximately 14 hours. This is quite a commitment. **KEY:** *Saving money does take work.*

For the week you pick, fill in the dates (for example, 9/15, 9/16, and so on). Make sure that you have clearly labeled the month and the dates/days that you are doing the grocery store study. As I said, this exercise lasts seven consecutive days; do not miss any days during the week that you select to do it.

After selecting your week, then choose two different grocery stores. Choose only full-service grocery stores. Circle Ks, 7-Elevens and mom-and-pop stores are out. Also, do not use any store that requires a membership fee. This eliminates such stores as Sam's Club and Costco, to name two.

(There is nothing wrong with convenience stores or stores requiring a membership, but please do not use them for your comparisons.)

Once you have chosen two supermarkets to compare, make a list of items for which you plan to compare the prices. Then, visit the stores, and take your copy of the Comparative Shopper Worksheet with you. Remember: You are not to buy the stuff. You are only doing a comparative price check.

Make sure that you select the same item at each store (i.e., the same brand name, size, weight, etc.). This will make it possible for you to make true comparisons at the end of each day and at the end of the week. You may also discover the days that prices go up or down. This will give you the opportunity to see if the ups and downs of your grocery store agree with what is suggested at the beginning of this section.

Caution: You will *not* need a cart to do this exercise. Remember! You are only at these stores to compare the different prices of the staples on the shelves. Do not load up a cart, as one former student reported doing. Just compare!

Upon completing the Comparative Shopper Exercise, write a statement using the space below (approximately 50 words) about what you learned from it. In your answer, consider the following: Of the two stores you compared, did you find one to be more expensive than the other? Were there any price changes on a daily basis? What percentage difference did you find between the stores that you compared? Did either of the stores have a sale during your comparison week? Did you notice that either store changed their prices on specific days? If you didn't, then check to see which dates featured higher prices, lower prices, or unchanged prices. Did you know that some grocery stores raise their prices according to the pay period schedule of the communities in which they do business? There is a lot to learn about shopping and saving money at the grocery store. What did *you* learn from

exercise

doing this exercise?

_____

_____

_____

_____

_____

KEY: *Be aware of the paydays in your area.* They may be on the 1st, 5th, 10th, or 25th of the month. A day or two before and after these dates, prices on store shelves may be higher than other days of the month. Experience has shown that prices of certain products can vary as much as 5

Name _____   Week of _____

Store A _____   Store B _____

GROCERY STORE COMPARATIVE SHOPPER EXERCISE														Side One
DAY	SUN		MON		TUES		WED		THURS		FRI		SAT	
DATE														
THE STORE	A	B	A	B	A	B	A	B	A	B	A	B	A	B
GROCERY LIST														
Beverages														
Coffee														
Tea														
Milk														
Cereal														
1.														
2.														
3.														
Freezer—Meat/Veg.														
1.														
2.														
3.														
4.														
Produce														
1.														
2.														
3.														
4.														
Subtotal														
< - > and < + >														
THE STORE	A	B	A	B	A	B	A	B	A	B	A	B	A	B

GROCERY STORE COMPARATIVE SHOPPER EXERCISE														Side Two	
DAY	SUN		MON		TUES		WED		THURS		FRI		SAT		
DATE															
THE STORE	A	B	A	B	A	B	A	B	A	B	A	B	A	B
GROCERY LIST															
Dairy Products															
1.															
2.															
3.															
Laundry Products															
1.															
2.															
3.															
Paper Products															
1.															
2.															
3.															
Desserts															
1.															
2.															
Other															
Other															
Other															
Other															
Subtotal															
< - > and < + >															
THE STORE	A	B	A	B	A	B	A	B	A	B	A	B	A	B

SAVE AND REDUCE

As you might suspect, I pride myself on rarely going to the store without coupons or purchasing goods that are not on sale. In fact, lately I have saved as much as 15% each month simply by using coupons. Combining the use of coupons with shopping at the right store at the right time has been a boon to my financial plan! If my family's grocery bill is between $400 and $500 per month, I reduce my cost by $60 to $75 by shopping cautiously and using coupons.

to 9%. Knowing where and when to shop can make a difference in spending wisely. Watch your money so you can save and invest the savings.

Coupons. "What about coupons?" you ask. **KEY:** *Whenever you shop, use coupons—but be careful. Some grocery chains accept coupons and even double or triple their face value, but their products are more expensive to begin with.* Get into the habit of shopping smart with coupons. Make it a point to check prices regularly to determine where it makes most sense to use your coupons. Using coupons can mean a savings of many dollars each month.

Sales. Watch for sales, of course, but again, be exceedingly cautious. For a store to declare a sale, it only has to have a few items on sale. The sale items, if you need them, can be a great buy, and if you can use a coupon as well, you can get even greater savings. Remember! The purpose of the sale from the store manager's point of view is to get you into the store. **KEY:** *Watch the cost of nonsale items when a sale is going on.* Often, the prices on nonsale items are raised from 2 to 5% to make up for the loss taken on the sale items, so what you saved on buying the sale item you lost on purchasing the nonsale item. I suggest you use your shopping list. Buy only those sale items identified on your list. Then leave the store.

Do you remember from Exhibit 4.2 how quickly $90 per month, when invested in a fund returning 10% annually, can become more than $300,000 in 30 years? Now you have an opportunity to add another $60 to $75 to your investment cash. You are becoming a wiser shopper by being aware of ways to avoid unnecessary spending.

Guarantees and Warranties

When you purchase a big-ticket item, often there is an option to purchase an extended warranty and/or guarantee for the item. It has been found that extended warranties and guarantees are unnecessary and therefore an unnecessary expense.

Dealers offer guarantees and warranties on repair and products. They can also sell extended guarantees and warranties. For most items—large and small—the manufacturer's warranty or guarantee on the item should be sufficient. (You may wish to make an exception and purchase an extended warranty for a big-ticket item, such as a car or a refrigerator, but usually the manufacturer's guarantee covers the product sufficiently.) Remember, the aim is to keep your money in your pocket. Check the manufacturer's guarantee and then decide whether to buy additional protection, but the finding has been that extended protection policies are high-priced insurance plans that you will not use.

KEY: *The guarantees and warranties that come with the products you purchase—even for car repair and replacement—are usually sufficient coverage, and the extended programs are not necessary.*

Of course, you must be your own judge as to whether to buy an extended warranty or guarantee, but most products fail within the first 90 to 180 days of purchase. Most warranties and guarantees cover this period of time, and some last even longer. Sometimes, it is less expensive to purchase a new product than to purchase the extended protection. And— here is food for thought—today, many products come with a lifetime guarantee. **KEY:** *Check your warranty or guarantee before buying any extended protection.* Know what you get when you buy the item, and then decide. Just know that extended warranties and guarantees can cost you unnecessary dollars.

If you want to learn more about warranties and guarantees, there are a variety of consumer protection websites. Two of my favorites are www.clarkhoward.com/ and www.troubleshooter.com/. Clark Howard and Tom Martino are nationally recognized consumer advocates and have syndicated call-in talk shows on which they offer a wealth of information to consumers. If you are still interested in purchasing an extended warranty or guarantee with that next purchase, invest a few moments at either of their websites.

Using the lines below, write a paragraph summarizing three or more things you learned from this section.

_____

_____

_____

_____

Debt and Credit Card Mismanagement

Are you aware that banks and credit card companies already have your name and address in their files? They wait for you to graduate from high school and to start college and then send you one of their credit cards. They want you to get into the habit of charging. For them, it is good business. For you, having a credit card can be a nightmare and can negatively impact your credit rating for long periods of time. If possible, don't charge!

KEY: *Avoid the enticement to charge. Using plastic costs money.*

There is nothing wrong with having a charge account or a credit card, provided you can keep it under control.

KEY: *A charge left unpaid at the end of a month can become a high-interest loan.* Many credit cards charge interest rates of 18 to 21% or higher on unpaid balances. This is money out of your pocket. At these rates, a credit card balance of $1,000 costs you an additional $180 to $210 each year. In essence, if you make only minimum payments, you are paying interest on the interest.

KEY: *Defer immediate gratification. Wait to make a purchase until you can pay with cash.* Think of what you could do with an extra $180 to $210 each year. You know my recommendation—invest it!

KEY: *The secret to using plastic to your advantage is to pay your card off, fully, each month.* That's right. Avoid leaving a balance on your credit card account. As I said, maintaining a balance, you are paying interest on the interest you are charged for the privilege of using the card. If you can pay the entire balance in one payment, go ahead and charge. Otherwise, my suggestion is to not charge at all. Instead, wait until you have the cash to buy the item you want.

It is estimated that more than 60% of college students own credit cards. A 2002 *CNNMoney* article (http://money.cnn.com/2002/03/08/college/q_studentdebt) reported that students leave college with large credit card debt and unmanageable debt levels. Even though many see a credit card as a convenience and as a useful tool, for some it can prove to be dangerous. Lazarony (June 5, 1998) reported that the average graduate has credit card debt of $2,200 and the figure jumps to $5,800 for graduate students. Many students do pace their credit card spending, but some are in over their heads. In fact, one of my students produced 36 cards that he reported regularly using and considered it an honor to have so many.

The following examples may be meaningful to you. I share the information to point out the dangers of becoming addicted to the thrill of using plastic. The stories are about two high school students who graduated in 1994: Rick K. and Jamie S.

Rich K. was an average student who graduated from the local high school in the middle of his class. He was planning to attend the local community college. A month before his high school graduation, he received an unrequested application for a credit card with a credit line of $1,500. To get the credit card, all he had to do was sign the application and mail it back in the self-addressed, postage-paid envelope. Easy! He signed it. By the end of June, only three weeks after his graduation, he had charged over $1,200 on the card. Rich K's summer job earned him take-home pay (after deductions) of around $108 per week. That doesn't sound bad, but Rich K. soon found out how expensive a 19.9% interest charge could be each month.

Jamie S. graduated with high honors from her high school. She had a full scholarship to a top university. From the summer of her graduation until she began study in the fall, Jamie received not *one* unrequested credit card, but *twelve*. Each card had a credit line of from $2,500 to $5,000. Jamie had no summer job or plans for one. Instead, she took two college courses at the local community college to earn some credits for advanced standing at the university. She did not plan to work once at the university, either. She expected that her scholarship would provide for her needs and most of her expenses. She was also lulled into thinking that her family would help take care of her remaining financial needs. Wrong! By the end of the second month of her first semester, Jamie was more than $35,000 in debt.

As further reported by Vega in his article, "Credit card issuers started targeting students after the market for new credit card holders became saturated less than a decade ago." From the issuers' standpoint, it was a sound business strategy: Of the student cardholders arriving on campus each semester, 67% of them stick with their first card. Statistically, credit card companies found that these students were less of a credit risk than the general adult population. This is great if you are one of the 67%. What about the remaining 33% that have difficulty handling credit?

This practice continues to be problematic. It has become even worse since credit card companies and banks started paying institutions of higher education a fee for providing them with the names of new students. Credit card companies continue to send out their unsolicited cards. Unfortunately, they will entice other new students who, like Rich K. and Jamie S., consider the credit cards to be a ticket to "free money."

 KEY: *A credit card is a high-interest loan when not paid off monthly.* Teenagers and adults alike need to take credit cards for what they are: easy access to loan funds, *not* access to free money.

Back to Rich K. and Jamie S. What became of them? Because Rich K. continued his job part-time while he attended the local community college, he found it possible to make his payments. However, after one year of not using the card but still having interest added onto the principal, he still owed almost $1,000.

Jamie S., on the other hand, did not have as much luck. She found herself forced to withdraw from the university, give up her full scholarship, and get a job. However, without a college degree she could only get a job paying a little better than minimum wage. At the end of one year, she filed for bankruptcy, because she was unable to keep up with the high credit card payments and defaulted on each of her cards. This will likely have a negative impact on her credit for the rest of her life.

On the brighter side, Jamie S. did eventually return to college part-time and took a full-time job. It took her six years to earn her bachelor's degree from the local college. She now realizes that for her a credit card is addictive. When she gets one in the mail, she cuts it up. **KEY:** *Cut up any unrequested credit or bank cards that you receive through the mail.*

Perhaps you are having a hard time believing these stories. "This will never happen to me," you are thinking. Unfortunately, credit card companies see targeting students as good business, and they will continue this practice. As a result, you could become a victim of too many credit cards and too much credit. It is easy to turn credit into debt. An August 2002 *Young Money* article reported that people—especially students—are vulnerable to overextending their credit regardless of background or income level.

KEY: *Use your credit card as a last resort and only if you know you can pay the full amount charged in one payment at the end of the month.*

If you must use a credit card and you expect to take a longer period to repay the debt, compare interest rates. Obtain rate information from multiple financial services firms to get the best value for your money. A website that offers interest rate comparisons is: www.eyeoncredit.com/. This site has

NEW RULES ARE ON THE HORIZON FOR CREDIT CARD ENTICERS

Colleges and universities are seeking a halt to the release of student names to credit card companies, according to Natalie Patton of the *Las Vegas Review–Journal* (Friday, January 11, 2002, p. 1B).

The chancellor of the University and Community College of Southern Nevada, Dr. Jane Nichols, states, "The rate of student debt is increasing nationally. We do not want in any way to appear to be doing anything that would encourage students to go further into debt." (*Las Vegas Review–Journal,* Friday, January 11, 2002.)

Even though colleges and universities receive sizable monetary stipends from the credit card companies—often based on how many students sign up and the amount of the charges made by these students—they will increasingly follow the lead of Chancellor Nichols and UCCSN and cease this practice. (As reported by Patton, the two southern Las Vegas institutions received $16,000 and $100,000 from credit card companies in 2001.)

Fortunately, under the leadership of Dr. Nichols, the entire university and community college system of Nevada will cease providing students' names to credit card companies. They will be doing the right thing.

a marketplace of credit cards. Try it! You can find other sites for this purpose on the Internet. All you need do is look.

Too Many Credit Cards, Too Much Debt

There is help! Facing a stack of bills week after week can be a very frustrating experience. Perhaps you have six or more credit cards and are maxed out on each one, with an accumulated debt of between $15,000 and $38,000 (Ramsey, 1997). Families just like yours have gotten into this dangerous buy-now, pay-later syndrome. Many people begin their credit debt when still in high school and college. Others are just addicted to the having-it-now syndrome, find they can't wait, and then find it difficult to pay more than the minimum each month. Yet others may not have known about credit card interest rates and penalty fees.

The things _not_ to do. First, _avoid borrowing from your retirement fund account_ to pay off your credit-card debt. Some 401(k) accounts allow you to borrow one half of what you have in your account up to $50,000. The purpose of your retirement account is for retirement, however. Find another source for paying off your debts.

Second, _do not get a lower interest card,_ you know, the ones that keep coming in the mail unsolicited. Get rid of the cards you never requested; cut them up immediately. **KEY:** _If you have more than one credit card, keep one and cut up all the others._ Your goal is to pay off your credit cards. You cannot do this by continuing to charge.

You are not alone. There is help.

The things you _can_ do. First, contact each of your credit card companies and _attempt to renegotiate your debt_ through reduced payments with reduced interest or reduced payments with no interest.

Second, if you own your home and have equity in it, you might consider consolidating your debt by _refinancing your mortgage_ and taking cash out or by _obtaining a home equity loan._ Both of these options have the advantage of being tax-deductible. Usually, you will find that the interest rate on the second mortgage will be less—possibly even less than half—the interest rate on your credit card.

Third, _borrow money from a family member_ to reduce or eliminate your debt. It is important to be responsible if you do this—do not take your debt and pass it on to a generous family member. Be very clear that this is a loan and not a gift. Arrange a repayment plan with your family benefactor. It would be appropriate to accept the loan and pay a low interest rate until the full debt is paid off.

Fourth, _cut up all but one of your credit cards._ Get rid of all store charge accounts, as well. The credit card that you hold on to is for airplane, hotel,

When you maintain a debt on your credit card, you have 25 days to make your payments, but when you pay your card off monthly, you are given only 20 days.

and other travel necessities, but it is never to be used instead of cash or for impromptu purchases. Also, you need to make sure that what you charge can be paid off in full within 20 days.

Last, *cut your expenses.* Track your spending and your household expenses for a few months. See what you can eliminate. Besides cutting up your credit cards, this is probably the quickest road to debt reduction.

Use the Estimated Yearly Household Operating Budget (Exhibit A.5 in the appendix) to help you to make these decisions, or go online to www.dinkytown.net/personal.html/ to find the personal financial calculator.

Using the lines below, write a paragraph summarizing three or more things you learned from this section.

exercise

_____

_____

_____

_____

Getting Credit Card or Debt Counseling

If none of the five suggestions just given work for you, you can contact a nonprofit debt counseling agency. This type of organization can work for you—its number one goal is to help you to climb out of debt.

One of the leaders in this field is the National Foundation for Credit Counseling (NFCC). In 2000 alone, the NFCC counseled 1.6 million American households through its 1,450 centers. Even people you might not expect—lawyers and judges, financial planners and CPAs—seek help in eliminating personal debt.

Many people fall into debt as a result of a life-changing event, such as a job loss, death in the family, illness, or divorce. Whatever brought you to the point of debt, it quickly becomes apparent that you cannot pay off the debt with a lump sum payment at the end of the month.

Although the NFCC and its brother and sister organizations are ethical, others are not. Unfortunately, there are some not-so-honorable companies that seek to profit from your desperation and employ high-pressure sales tactics to get you to sign with them. Many offer little more than a quick road to bankruptcy court, which should always be a last resort.

 Be cautious! Check the details before you sign anything. If you are in debt today, waiting until tomorrow will not change your situation very much. **KEY:** *Wait until you are fully informed before signing up with a debt counseling company.*

I would suggest looking up the NFCC on the Internet. It is located at www.nfcc.org/. Two other sources of credit counseling assistance are Atlanta-based Consumer Credit Counseling at www.cccsatl.org/ and Consumer Credit Counseling of Orlando at www.cccssoutheast.org/. Or you can look up credit counseling services in your own city in your yellow pages phone directory. Before contacting an organization you find in the phone directory, contact your local Better Business Bureau.

Despite the fact that there are unethical debt counselors, you will find that there are plenty of reputable organizations out there as well, who are willing to help you negotiate a manageable repayment schedule and identify areas of overspending. Finding a good credit-counseling program can be a bit tricky, however. As with so many other things, you have to study and prepare.

1. Look for a nonprofit firm. You have spent too much already; why pay more now? Nonprofits get most of their funding from creditors, not you. The nonprofits' relationship with those in debt is beneficial in that they can often negotiate better rates than you could with your creditors. Some nonprofits may ask for a nominal fee or suggest that you give a donation to enroll. You can decide whether you want to contribute or to look for another organization.

2. Privacy isn't usually an issue, but it's wise to check on the agency's policy.

3. Make sure the agency does not sell your information to other organizations.

4. Find out up front exactly what services you will receive—the more the better. Services might include counseling, a debt-repayment plan, and budgeting advice. You might want to have it all in writing before you proceed.

5. Ask if the organization belongs to any professional groups, such as the NFCC or the Better Business Bureau.

6. Ask the counselor to explain the company's auditing process and the means of protecting your funds. You are putting your money in their hands, after all.

7. This is the big one: Put together all your bills, and take them with you to the credit counselor you have selected. He will figure out what you owe

and work with you to determine how much you can pay each month. Then, instead of writing checks to each creditor, you will write one to the service, which will then distribute the money. The goal is to develop a plan that allows you to afford the necessities of life (and even the occasional movie) and at the same time whittle away at the balances you owe.

Here is what should happen.

1. If you have been receiving phone calls from creditors, these should stop within three to six weeks. A few persistent creditors may call after this time, but if so, calmly tell them that you are working with a debt counseling agency and give them the credit counselor's phone number. This usually causes the phone calls to stop.

2. Your credit counselor should talk to creditors and try to get them to reduce your interest rates and waive late fees to shorten the length of time you are in debt. Today, interest rates on credit cards are at an all-time low—9% as opposed to 18% or 21%. Better yet, your counselor may also coax creditors to "re-age" your account—that is, report past due amounts as current.

3. Credit counselors can achieve these arrangements because most creditors are glad to see you enrolling in a repayment program and agreeing to pay a little at a time rather than heading for bankruptcy court—even if it will take several years. If those creditors were to enlist the services of a collection agency, the agency would take perhaps half of whatever it recovered.

All this may put you on your way to debt freedom—but maybe not. Old habits may be hard to break. To say out of debt, you need to change your spending habits. No one can do this for you. Are you ready for a new class—Budgeting 101?

Budgeting 101: Getting By Without "Plastic"

This may be the best class you will ever enroll in. You are now ready to change your life and your family's future financial situation. You are on your way to paying off your old debt. Now, you'll need to set up a budget. People who use plastic can tend to avoid budgeting and money management. But it is a necessity!

Your credit counselor can help with this, but you need to take charge as well. Make it a habit to know how much you spend each day and each month. Know about the big-ticket items, the rent or mortgage payments, and the utility bills. Don't lose track of how much you spend on extras, either—snacking, restaurants, dry cleaners, and toys, to name a few.

Plastic can obscure your view of how much you are spending and what's left in your pocket. You need to get a clearer picture of what you actually have and what you want. To do this, you will need to plan and set goals.

How can you prevent your debt history from repeating itself? In Budgeting 101, you must accept the responsibility for planning. You need to plan not to use plastic and to purchase only necessities. Wanting something does not make its purchase a necessity. There is a difference between "need" and "want." Do the exercise that follows to help distinguish between the two.

The Budgeting Plan 101 Quiz is designed to help you defer "But I want it" (and thus be able to devote more money to necessities and investment) by carefully considering certain questions. Thinking about these questions may stop you from giving in to the temptation to make a questionable purchase. After completing the quiz, you will realize that you are in control of whether to buy or not to buy. Remember! The budget does not control you. *You* are in control of your budget.

BUDGETING PLAN 101 QUIZ: BUYING ONLY NECESSITIES

Directions: Check a response of Yes or No. Fill in information where requested.

1. Do I need the item I want to buy? ❑ **Yes** ❑ **No**
   If **yes,** then write a justification for the expense, and go to Question 2.

   _____

   _____

   _____

   If **no,** don't buy it.

2. Can I easily substitute something I already have? ❑ **Yes** ❑ **No**
   If **no,** continue to Question 3. If **yes,** don't buy it.

3. Can I buy it used or recycled for less money, or even arrange a trade? ❑ **Yes** ❑ **No**
   If **no,** continue to Question 4. If **yes,** look into acquiring the item second hand or bartering for it.

4. Is it exactly what I want, so that I won't have to change or replace it soon? ❑ **Yes** ❑ **No**
   If it's exactly what you want, continue to Question 5. If it's not exactly what you want, then don't buy it until you've had a chance to look around more.

5. If I wait three months, will I still want it? ❑ **Yes** ❑ **No**
   If **yes,** continue to Question 6. If **no,** consider carefully whether it's worth it.

6. Will owning it make me happier or make my life better? ❑ **Yes** ❑ **No**
   If your answer is **yes,** then *buy it!* If your answer is **no,** however, take a deep breath, walk away, and be proud of your restraint.

A Method for Avoiding Credit Card Debt

Here is a very easy and special way to keep your credit card spending under check. To keep credit card spending under check is to pay your credit card bill off monthly. Do you not believe that you can do this? Read on! The price of this book is worth this **KEY** alone: *When you use your credit card, take out your checkbook, and instead of writing a check number in the space, write "CC" in small letters. Record the date and place where you made the charge in the appropriate columns. Subtract the credit card charge from your checking account balance. Keep going! In the Fee column, put a slash mark (/). Then wait for your credit card statement to arrive. When it does, go through your checkbook and identify all the CC recordings you have made (see next page).*

Ck No.	Date	Transaction Description	Payment/Debit		Code	Fee	Deposit/Credit		Balance 3,275.33	
467	1/17	Mortgage Payment	1,188	76					2,086	57
CC	1/18	Gas—Martin Station	19	65	/				2,066	92
468	1/18	College Tuition—BMI U	786	50					1,280	42
CC	1/18	College Textbooks—BMI U	355	74	/				924	68
469	1/18	Consumer Utilities	93	43					831	25
Deposit	1/19	Payment from Work					997	53	1,828	78
470	1/19	Peter's Dry Cleaning	23	33					1,805	45

Write out one check to your credit card company to cover all the charges made, and under each of the CC notes put the check number of that one check. You now have a record of which check you used to pay for all of those charges. (Don't double charge yourself—just write out the check, but do not subtract the amount from your balance; you already did that.) There is one last thing to do. Look in your checkbook and over each slash mark, make a slash going the other way (\). Your mark will then look like an X. This is a quick way to show you have paid for this charge.

Your checkbook will look something like the following chart:

Ck No.	Date	Transaction Description	Payment/Debit		Code	Fee	Deposit/Credit		Balance 3,275.33	
467	1/17	Mortgage Payment	1,188	76					2,086	57
CC 471	1/18	Gas—Martin Station	19	65		X			2,066	92
468	1/18	College Tuition—BMI U	786	50					1,280	42
CC 471	1/18	College Textbooks—BMI U	355	74		X			924	68
469	1/18	Consumer Utilities	93	43					831	25
Deposit	1/19	Payment from Work					997	53	1,828	78
470	1/19	Peter's Dry Cleaning	23	33					1,805	45
471	123	MC or VISA Payment	[375	79]					1,805	45

If you follow this method, there is no reason for you to misuse your credit card. In addition, you will find that you will be paying off your credit card in full, each month.

Avoid falling back into your old patterns of spending. It may not be easy, but you will find that the rewards will outweigh the restrictions that to some degree are placed upon you. The rewards are nothing less than having your plans and goals met and being able to support yourself and your family in your nonworking years.

You can take a chance and again use credit unwisely, or you can choose to be a wise consumer. In the final analysis, the choice is yours.

Some Final Thoughts on Credit Cards

KEY: *Be careful how you use your credit.* All that glitters may turn out to be fool's gold. It is best to wait until you have the cash before making a major purchase, except for *very* major items like a home or a car. Your rule of thumb should be not to borrow what you can't repay in 20 days.

If you borrow to pay off credit card debt, be a responsible borrower who repays as promised, showing you are worthy of getting credit in the future. Before you borrow, compare your total payment obligations with the income you will have available to make these payments. Your credit past is your credit future. Credit bureaus maintain credit reports, which contain a borrower's history of repaying loans. Negative information in your credit report can affect your ability to borrow later—for instance, when you want to purchase a house.

Think of credit cards this way: Under control they are a luxury, but like a drug, they can be addictive when abused. They have the potential to be destructive to you and your ability to save for the future. So be careful.

With improved habits, you are on your way to living without debt, but failure is only a charge away. I trust you will get your credit report clean, and with a clean credit record, credit card lenders will besiege you with offers. This is a good sign, if you have learned to manage your money. It can be devastating if you have only pretended to meet your goals. Be aware that it is easy to fall back on old behaviors, so try to avoid doing so at all costs.

TREASURE CHEST
E X E R C I S E

Using the lines below, write a short summary of what you learned as a result of reading this chapter. Make it a point to list at least *three* **KEYS** in your writing. Indicate clearly how you expect to use these KEYS to guide your financial life.

_____

_____

_____

_____

_____

_____

_____

_____

_____

_____

_____

_____

_____

_____

_____

_____

_____

_____

_____

_____

5

SUCCESSFUL FINANCIAL PLANNING

Setting Up a Financial Plan

Write a financial goal/plan using the lines below.

_____

_____

_____

_____

Is this goal believable and obtainable within a specific amount of time? Is it something you really want? Can you control it, and adapt it, if necessary? If you are setting a goal for your family, get your family members to help create the goal. If you are a single teenager or young student living at home, get your family involved with this activity. **KEY:** *For a family goal to work, it must be the creation of the entire family.* The family must believe in it and want it as much as you do. If just one member does not accept the goal, it can mean disaster for your financial plan.

A good first step in involving family members is to take a piece of paper and write down everything you all spend. Include change—it can add up to more than you think. Record what you spend, down to the small items, such as the newspaper, bagel with cream cheese, and mocha latte you grab on your way to work. (Hint: Eat at home, if possible. It's cheaper.)

To help you, I provide worksheets on the pages that follow and in the appendix. These charts are similar to those used in running a business. Use them to keep track of your spending and to help you to budget.

The best money managers set goals, track the money coming in and going out, and create a wise plan for investing. They don't just arbitrarily spend. It is now your opportunity to take control of your money and spending.

Mapping Out Your Financial Future

Take time to list your financial goals and a realistic plan for achieving them. Again, if it's a plan for the family, you must include all members. You can go places you want to go without a roadmap, but seldom on the first try. As one writer wrote, "If you don't know where you're going, you'll probably end up somewhere else" (Campbell, 1990). I cannot overstate the need for having a plan and a map to accomplish this plan. Too often people set out on trips but never get to where they wanted to go because they did not have a plan.

The following is a series of steps you might consider in developing your map to a successful financial future.

1. Assess your current financial picture. Make a list of all your assets and your debts. Use Exhibit 5.1 to help you figure out your current financial picture.

Study the budget worksheet you just filled out. Work with it. Make a copy of it. Another copy appears in the appendix (Exhibit A.3). Are there expenses that occur more or less often than once a month? If so, convert them to a monthly amount when calculating the monthly budget. For instance, if an insurance expense is billed every six months, you would convert it to a monthly amount by dividing the six-month premium by six.

2. Determine your short-, mid-, and long-term financial goals. Write down the things you hope to accomplish financially in each of these time ranges, and group them according to when you will need the money. Examples might be saving for your next vacation (a short-term goal), building a college fund for yourself (a mid-term goal), or planning for your retirement needs (a long-term goal). (Be sure to include the retirement goal, regardless of your age. Planning for retirement is a lifetime commitment.)

3. Develop a realistic plan for accomplishing your goals. Figuring out how much you'll need for all future goals can be difficult. With a specific vision you can accomplish this, however. Avoid becoming sidetracked through lack of focus.

4. Change your money priorities. This is a crucial step: Change your attitude toward money. Stop living for immediate gratification and replace that with a desire to plan for tomorrow.

	BUDGET WORKSHEET.	**EXHIBIT 5.1**	

CATEGORY	MONTHLY BUDGET AMOUNT	MONTHLY ACTUAL AMOUNT	DIFFERENCE
INCOME: Wages Paid, Misc.			
EXPENSES:			
Rent/Mortgage			
All Utilities			
Cable/Internet/TV			
Telephone			
Home Repairs/Maintenance			
Car Payments			
Gasoline/Oil			
Auto Repairs/Maintenance, Fees, etc.			
Other Transportation Costs			
Auto Insurance			
Child Care			
Home Owners'/Renters' Insurance			
Computer Expenses			
Groceries			
Eating Out			
Credit Cards Expense			
Other			
EXPENSES SUBTOTAL			
NET INCOME (Income Less Expenses)			

5. Learn the basics of personal finance.

a. Debts you pay in installments (such as automobile loans, credit cards, store charge accounts, personal loans, or student loans) should not exceed 20% of your annual take-home pay. If your debt payments exceed 20%, you are overextended in credit obligations.

b. You need to have a cushion of from three to six months of your annual take-home pay, for short-term emergencies or lower-income months.

c. Mid- and long-term savings needs will depend on the goals you developed in Step 2, above.

6. Find the best financial products.

    a. Credit, savings, and investment products change every day, and new products are always emerging. Do your homework and learn more about different offerings. Shop around to find the products that are best-suited to your unique circumstances, spending patterns, savings and investment objectives, and lifestyle.

    b. Be sure to take advantage of all the well-suited investment and savings options that are available to you. If you are working, one of the best ones would be your employer's retirement program. Many employers will make a match equal to your contribution to the retirement fund up to a certain maximum. This type of investment grows tax deferred until you retire. Also, if you are eligible for a Roth IRA, take advantage of this option.

7. Put your plan on autopilot through automatic deposits.

    a. Save money for your investments and retirement first.

    b. Minimize the chance of derailing your plan by arranging to have money automatically deposited into your accounts. Sign an agreement with your employer to have money deducted from your paycheck and deposited into your retirement and other savings accounts—before you even see the money. These amounts will grow pre-taxed.

These steps represent just the beginning. Learn more about budgeting by going to the following website: http://parentingteens.com/lifeskills5.shtml.

Using the lines below, write a paragraph summarizing three or more things you learned from this section.

_____

_____

_____

_____

_____

Making a Financial Plan a Family Affair

Begin at once to make your and your family's financial goal into a reality. Stop making excuses that you are not ready. Remember, each journey begins with a single step. Take that first step today by completing this exercise about your financial goal.

FINANCIAL GOAL

My/our financial goal/plan is to: [Restate the goal you wrote in Chapter 1. If it needs revising, do so now. If this is a family plan, make certain that all members of the family agree with it. State your goal as follows: "I/we plan . . ." or "I/we will . . ." Never say, "I will try . . ."

_____

_____

_____

State your timeframe clearly. Give yourself a definite date by which you will fulfill your plan.

Target Date: I/we plan to have my/our financial goal/plan achieved by

day_____ month_____ year_____ at (time)_____

It is very important to be specific about when you plan to achieve your goal.

Consequences for Not Attaining My/Our Financial Goal: [*Be honest with yourself. Admit what the cost or loss would be to you and/or your family if you do not achieve this financial goal.*]

If I/we do not attain my/our financial goal, I/we would experience the following costs and losses:

_____

_____

_____

Can you accept these?   ❑ Yes   ❑ No   [*If this is a real goal, you cannot accept anything less than success.*]

Gains Associated with Attaining My/Our Financial Goal: [*Consider what gains may be in store for you if you achieve your financial goal.*]

The gains that I/we would experience if I/we achieve my/our financial goal are:

_____

_____

_____

Don't the gains make the financial goal even more desirable?   ❑ Yes   ❑ No

Next, focus on your assets by going to Exhibit A.2 in the appendix and filling out the Assets vs. Debits Balance sheet. It will help you better understand where your money is going. In addition, you may also find Exhibits A.3, A.4, A.5, and A.6 to be helpful. Also, fill out Exhibit 5.2.

KEY: *Read your financial goal/plan aloud, twice daily—once just before bed and once first thing in the morning. Make it a ritual for the family to recite at breakfast and dinner.* As you read and reread your goal statement, see, feel, and believe yourself already in possession of the goal. What you believe and how you feel determines how you act. How you act controls the outcome of your goal. Therefore, when you think about it and plan it, you can achieve it, because you are in control.

The Best Plan Is Kind and Gentle: Rethinking the Plan

Budgets are not villains, nor are financial plans. Both are goals set by you and your family to achieve something you desire. Accomplishment of the goals will be the result of the hard work from everyone in the family.

KEY: *Do not point fingers at anyone for a financial problem. It is truly a family affair.*

EXHIBIT 5.2	ASSETS VS. EXPENSE SHEET.			
ASSETS	**AMOUNT**	**EXPENSES**		**AMOUNT**
INCOME (all sources)		EXPENSES		
List:		All Credit Cards		
		All Store Charges		
		Household Expenses (itemized)		
		1.		
		2.		
		3.		
		4.		
		5.		
		6.		
		Miscellaneous Expenses		
TOTAL Assets		TOTAL Assets – Expenses =		
		NET WORTH		

Look again at the goal statement that you created, then revised in this chapter. Make sure you have narrowed it down to achievable goals. The goals should not be too large or too confusing. You may not be able to achieve every financial goal you've ever dreamed of, but you can achieve the most important ones if you identify them clearly and decide which are the most important. Then you can achieve them one at a time. You accomplish this by establishing priorities, as described in the following list.

1. *Focus on the goals that are the most meaningful to you first.* To accomplish primary goals, you will need to put equally desirable but less important ones on a back burner. It is helpful to classify goals as A, B, or C level. Work on your A-level goals first. Leave B and C goals for later.

2. *Be aware that your goals may conflict with each other.* When faced with a conflict between goals of equal importance, you need to find a way to choose between them. The nice thing is that if you decide that Goal 1 is more important that Goal 2, but you find yourself working on Goal 2, you may discover that you were wrong and that Goal 2 is really more important. There is nothing wrong with being flexible and deciding that Goal 2 is now more important. **KEY:** *In setting goals and managing money, don't write anything in blood.* Be willing to switch priorities if you realize that your choice of goals was incorrect. Here are some things to consider in establishing priorities:

　　a. Will my choice hurt anyone that I care about?

　　b. Will one choice benefit more people in my family than another?

　　c. Will a goal be hurt if it is deferred?

3. *As ever, plan early!* Early planning is a necessity for meeting significant goals like preparing for retirement or setting money aside for a child's or your own college fund. The reason for this is that money—whether it is invested in savings, stocks, bonds, or mutual funds—over time can grow substantially, but it *does* take time.

4. *Choose your goals carefully.* Make sure that the goals you select will help you to achieve financial security and give you a sense of enjoyment and accomplishment. This is an important consideration in deciding how to rank your different financial choices.

The following is a sample list of goals you might consider.

_____ Sufficient money in savings to handle an emergency

_____ Sufficient money to purchase a home or a larger home

_____ Sufficient money to get out of debt and stay there

_____ Sufficient money to invest with the aim of becoming financially independent

_____ Sufficient money to ensure that parents are taken care of in their senior years

_____ Sufficient money to send children to the college of their choice with no worry about debt

If none of the above seem to apply to you, make it a point to write down a few of your own.

_____

_____

_____

5. *Remember: Financial plans only succeed when all family members are involved.* Leave no one out of developing the plan. If grandparents live with you, they need to be included, too.

6. *Begin early.* This is different from plan early, from item number 3. The longer you wait to identify and begin working toward your goals, the more difficulty you'll have reaching them.

7. *Monitor your spending behavior—keep your spending on course.* Watch especially your spending on big ticket items. If you are wondering about buying something, ask yourself this question: "Will this take me nearer to my primary goals or lead me farther away from them?" If an expense—especially a big purchase—won't get you closer to your goals, make every effort to defer it or just not buy it.

8. *Watch your spending on small items, too.* Although I encourage you to defer or avoid big-ticket expenses and keep yourself focused on your long-range plans, most of your expenses are those things that nickel and dime you. As long as you provide for your long-range needs, then enjoy yourself, but don't let your expenses get away from you. The most important thing is to always keep that long-range goal in mind.

9. *Change is inevitable.*

    a. Be prepared to update your goals when circumstances change.

    b. Your needs and desires will probably change as you age, so you should probably reexamine your goals and priorities yearly.

    c. Review your goals regularly to be certain they are still the ones you want. To accomplish this, you will need to picture the goal clearly in your mind and keep it written down in detail.

TREASURE CHEST

E X E R C I S E

Using the lines below, write a short summary of what you learned as a result of reading this chapter. Make it a point to list at least *three* KEYS in your writing. Indicate clearly how you expect to use these KEYS to guide your financial life.

_____

_____

_____

_____

_____

_____

_____

_____

_____

_____

_____

_____

_____

_____

_____

_____

_____

_____

_____

_____

_____

_____

6

FINANCIAL FREEDOM

BUDGETING AND MEETING YOUR GOALS

Do you think you are ready to create a budget? Are you ready to change your spending habits to meet your and your family's specific goals? You have given much thought to planning; now you need to give similar thought to your spending. The more care you put into creating your budget, the better the chance you will create one that will work for you.

Creating a budget requires planning. Planning will be made easier if you know how you have spent your money over the last 12 months. Knowing your spending habits helps you design an accurate budget that will allow you to meet your goals.

You do not have to wonder how certain people have learned how to amass great sums of money. The secret to accomplishing this lies in the willingness to plan. People who have achieved financial independence have learned how to plan.

KEY: *The first strategy for achieving financial independence is careful planning.* This idea is not new—it has been stated and restated in this book. You must know how you have spent money in the past so you can change or improve upon this pattern and save and invest for the future. **KEY:** *The second strategy for achieving financial independence is to save and invest the dollars you earn today for use tomorrow.*

Financial planning allows you to take control of your finances. "Yeah," you may be saying, "I can't think about financial planning. I barely have the money to buy shoes or gas for the car, or for helping my children finance a new home." **KEY:** *It does not matter what your past or current financial situation is. Financial planning is for everyone: children, teens, men, and women—all ages, ethnicities, nationalities, and backgrounds.*

You need to start managing your money now, while you are still able to form or modify your spending habits. If you make a habit of taking charge of your finances, your life will become more satisfying. **KEY:** *Planning today for tomorrow is the only way to free yourself of financial concerns in the future.*

Know Where You Are Financially

Financial planning is about assessing where you are now and where you want to go. Once you have set your goals (as described in Chapter 5), you then have an idea of how to achieve them. Every successful business—big and small—has a financial plan (that is, a budget) so it can get the most out of each dollar. Consider your personal money management to be like running a business.

Not only must a business know where its money is going, it needs to know all its sources of revenue. Similarly, you need to know about your household revenue. Complete the Estimated Budget of Resources/Income worksheet (Exhibit 6.1) in preparation for doing the monthly household budget. Remember to include money coming in from all sources.

Good! The next step is to calculate where the revenue is going. In Exhibit 6.2, Estimated Average Monthly/Yearly Family Expense Budget, add up your average estimated monthly expenses. Be as accurate as possible. Later you will fill out a more detailed budget (Exhibit 6.3), which will in all probability be more accurate. For now, make your best possible estimate.

EXHIBIT 6.1	ESTIMATED BUDGET OF FAMILY RESOURCES/INCOME.

Prepared as of (Date)	
SOURCE	**ESTIMATED AMOUNT PER MONTH**
Income—Self (full-time)	$
Income—Self (part-time)	$
Spouse's Income	$
Parental Contribution	$
Savings	$
Investments	$
Other	$

ESTIMATED AVERAGE MONTHLY/YEARLY FAMILY EXPENSE BUDGET.		EXHIBIT 6.2

Prepared as of (Date)

EXPENSE ITEM	ESTIMATED COST MONTHLY	ESTIMATED COST YEARLY
Housing: Rent/Mortgage	$	$
Car/Transportation	$	$
Health Insurance	$	$
Car Insurance	$	$
Utilities/Cable/Gas/Electric	$	$
Phone/Cell/Fax/Internet Line	$	$
Eating Out	$	$
Clothing	$	$
Food	$	$
Household Items	$	$
Laundry/Dry Cleaning	$	$
Healthcare	$	$
Recreation	$	$
Charges/Credit Cards	$	$
Repairs: Home, Auto, etc.	$	$
Other	$	$
	$	$
	$	$
	$	$
Total	$	$

Great! Next, take the information from these two forms and use them to calculate your detailed yearly household operating budget (Exhibit 6.3). Do this twice: once for the previous year, and once for the current year. You will find another copy of Exhibit 6.3 in the appendix (Exhibit A.5). Use that to make copies for your use. Regarding the budget for the previous year, even though you have receipts, it is still considered an estimate. Regarding the budget for the current year, do not estimate beyond 5 years. In goal set-

EXHIBIT 6.3	ESTIMATED YEARLY HOUSEHOLD OPERATING BUDGET.

Prepared as of (Date)		for												
		Jan.	Feb.	March	April	May	June	July	Aug.	Sept.	Oct.	Nov.	Dec.	Total
Fixed Payments	Total Income													
	Mortgage (rent)													
	Taxes													
	Insurance													
	Loans (Payments due to others)													
	Savings													
	Total Fixed Payments													
Flexible Payments	Utilities													
	House Improvements/ Repairs													
	Food													
	Clothing													
	Medical/Dental													
	Education													
	Recreation													
	Magazines/ Newspapers													
	Contributions													
	Automobile Expenditures													
	Credit Charges													
	Other													
	Total Flexible Payments													
Budget	Total Fixed and Flexible Payments													
	Total Income													
	Balance (+ or −)													

ting, goals further than 5 years into the future are considered long term. There is nothing wrong in having long-term goals, to give you direction, but a budget is meant to focus on a shorter term. For this exercise, restrict your estimated budgets to no more than five years ahead. After you complete this exercise, you can plan for the next 15 or more years, if you like. Many planners schedule 20 to 40 years ahead.

Notice that Exhibit 6.3 includes a section for some of the more usual *fixed expenses* (those expenses that remain the same each month). These include mortgage/rent, insurance premiums, and loans. The exhibit also includes a section for *flexible expenses* (those expenses that vary from month to month). These include utilities, home repairs, medical and dental expenses, magazines/newspapers, groceries, auto expenses, clothing, and entertainment. **KEY:** *Whenever possible, make savings a fixed expense.* In fact, make savings the budget item you pay first—either yourself or through a payroll deduction plan at your work.

Check the results of your calculations. What is your net worth (found on the Total column of the Balance row)? If your net worth is on the negative side, then delay adding to savings until your net worth is positive.

Note that, per this exercise, you need to have two yearly household operating budgets running concurrently: one for the previous year and one for the current year. It is also a good idea to make a proposed budget for next year.

The budget you create is for you and your family. You are creating it because you want to assure that your spending patterns will enable you to meet specific goals. The more care that you put into creating the budget, the better the chances are that you will create one that works for you.

Budgets can fail. When a budget fails, it is most often the case that the person or the family that created the budget did not set it up to reflect realistically how they want to live and spend money. This is why I insist that you know your own past spending history before you invest time in preparing a budget for the present or future.

All too often, a person's budgeted figures and actual figures are inconsistent. **KEY:** *The budget you prepare is not set in stone.* You need to be flexible and increase or decrease the amounts in your budget's line items until they are more accurate. For instance, you might find an additional resource that will cover an area that has been coming in over budget. The additional revenue will help you come within your budgeted parameters.

Remember: A budget is a tool for bringing your expenses in line with your income. When used properly, it can help you plan for important goals. The intent of a budget is to serve you and your goals. If you want to stick to a budget, it's important to create a reasonable one; otherwise, the frustration of always seeing the actual amount higher than the budgeted amount just might make you throw in the towel. **KEY:** *Create a realistic budget designed to fit your income and spending.* Once you see the overall picture of your spending habits, you might discover more restraint than you thought you had. Budgets—not money—can help you gain the discipline to refrain from indulging in all your impulses to spend.

Study your estimated yearly household operating budget for the current year one more time, and then take the Budgeting Plan 101 Review Quiz below. For every category in your budget, find a reason to keep your expenses to the amount you allotted. Consider the questions in the review quiz carefully the next time you are tempted to make a questionable purchase. Remember! The budget does not control you. *You* are in control of your budget.

BUDGETING PLAN 101 REVIEW QUIZ: BUYING ONLY NECESSITIES

Directions: Check a response of Yes or No. Fill in information where requested.

1. Do I need the item I want to buy?   ❏ **Yes**   ❏ **No**
   If **yes**, then write a justification for the expense, and go to Question 2.

   _____

   _____

   _____

   If **no**, don't buy it.

2. Can I easily substitute something I already have?   ❏ **Yes**   ❏ **No**
   If **no**, continue to Question 3. If **yes**, don't buy it.

3. Can I buy it used or recycled for less money, or even arrange a trade? ❏ **Yes**   ❏ **No**
   If **no**, continue to Question 4. If **yes**, look into acquiring the item second hand or bartering for it.

4. Is it exactly what I want, so that I won't have to change or replace it soon?   ❏ **Yes**   ❏ **No**
   If it's exactly what you want, continue to Question 5. If it's not exactly what you want, then wait until you've had a chance to look around more.

5. If I wait three months, will I still want it?   ❏ **Yes**   ❏ **No**
   If **yes**, continue to Question 6. If **no**, consider carefully whether it's worth it.

6. Will owning it make me happier or make my life better?   ❏ **Yes**   ❏ **No**
   If your answer is **yes**, then *buy it!* If your answer is **no**, however, take a deep breath, walk away, and be proud of your restraint.

TREASURE CHEST

E X E R C I S E

Using the lines below, write a short summary of what you learned as a result of reading this chapter. Make it a point to list at least *three* **KEYS** in your writing. Indicate clearly how you expect to use these KEYS to guide your financial life.

_____

_____

_____

_____

_____

_____

_____

_____

_____

_____

_____

_____

_____

_____

_____

_____

_____

_____

_____

7

ESTATE PLANNING

WILLS, PROBATE, AND OTHER LEGAL MATTERS

KEY: *You are never too young or too old to have a will.* There is no way to escape it. You must plan not only for the present and future, but also for the inevitable period beyond your own life. This chapter is devoted to the legal aspects of passing on your estate to your heirs. The material presented is general—for readers of all ages. When you decide to make a will, you need to work with an attorney. I am not an attorney. I have, however, experienced many of the situations I describe in this chapter. The following suggestions will hopefully make your death more acceptable to those whom you leave behind.

You worked hard all your life. You amassed some money and property—possibly more than you were able to spend during your lifetime. Thus, it is highly likely you will be leaving some sum of money and property to your heirs.

The passing on of your estate, and the eventual division of it among your heirs, can be a *dream* or a *nightmare*. Surprisingly, the choice is in your hands while you are alive as to which way it will go.

Before discussing probate, and wills, the discussion will first focus on other legal matters. The other legal matters can even be more of a nightmare than the other two topics.

Legal Documents to Support the Will

Do yourself, your family, and all your loved ones a favor by organizing each and every one of your legal documents. It is best to store them in a safe-deposit box, but many people today use a home file cabinet. One advantage of a file cabinet over a safe-deposit box is that often the bank seals your safe-deposit box immediately upon the date of the holder's death. If the will is in the box, your heirs may have difficulty getting it. On the other hand, the safe-deposit box may be the better choice because it is out of the house and not susceptible to household catastrophes such as fire, flood, or rain damage. To overcome the problem of the sealing of the safe-deposit box, arrange with the bank to make the box accessible to your executor. Also, grant him or her power of attorney upon your death. With this power assigned to the executor, the safe deposit concern is moot. In any case, make sure these papers are out of harm's way. Your family will be depending on you even in death.

What papers are there to consider? Besides the will, you need to have your marriage license, or licenses. If you have been divorced, you need to have the divorce papers. For some, this may mean multiple papers—one set for each divorce. If you served in any branch of the armed forces, it is good to keep your military discharge papers. You should also have the birth certificates (originals or copies) of your biological or adopted children. You also need to have titles and deeds to the home(s), car(s), boat(s), etc. that you own. Do you own rental property, stocks, bonds, or deeds of trust? Make it a point to store those away also. Lastly, do not forget your insurance policies.

Make sure that in your will you clearly name your *executor* or *executrix* (the person who will administer your estate). Think ahead and provide this person with knowledge about the location of all your documents, and if necessary, the keys to get to them. Many an executor has pulled out his hair trying to find the documents needed for probate. I do not mean to sound cold, but when passing on assets to the living, the state of residence of the deceased can be unsympathetic if documents are missing. It is a legal matter, and states want to see documents to support heirs' claims.

Again, be sure these documents are in order and in a place where they are easily retrievable.

The Will Administrator (Executor/Executrix)

It is not always necessary to have a will administrator. When necessary, however, an administrator can be worth their weight in gold. Therefore, you must give careful consideration to your choice of administrator. This person will have the responsibility of carrying out your requests in an impartial and diligent manner that is fair to all.

Realize how complex and demanding the job of an administrator is. The following list summarizes just some of the administrator's responsibilities in properly administering the will.

1. Arrange for probate of the will.

2. Obtain court authorization as the executor/executrix.

3. Post a bond for the faithful performance.

4. Transfer bank accounts to the account of the estate.

5. Take custody of securities and collect life insurance payable to the estate.

6. File claims for Social Security and/or veteran's benefits, and collect debts owed to the estate.

7. If the estate includes a going business, take steps to keep the business operating while arranging for the sale of its future continuation.

8. Locate and safeguard all other property belonging to the estate.

9. Make a complete and detailed inventory, and have all assets appraised.

10. Figure out how much money must be paid out in cash bequests, taxes, and other costs.

11. Decide what property has to be sold in order to raise cash and when to sell it.

12. Defend the estate against improper claims.

13. Pay all legitimate debts against the estate, and record all the receipts, transactions, and disbursements.

14. File a final income tax return for the deceased, and select a fiscal or calendar year for income tax purposes.

15. File income tax returns for the estate and a federal estate tax return, if appropriate and in keeping with current law.

16. If funds are available, pay bequests and legacies as directed by the will.

17. Make a final accounting to the court, and give notice thereof to all interested parties.

The list could go on. You can see how intricate the job of the administrator is and how much time, energy, and skill is demanded of this person. Lack of the necessary time may eliminate some excellent candidates from consideration. Although it is possible, do not expect that an inexperienced friend or relative will be able to learn this job as they go along. Put much thought and care into the selection of your administrator. **KEY:** *Select your administrator before death, and place the name of this person in your will.*

Probate of the Will

In the probate of your will, your executor or executrix goes to a probate court to show proof of the validity of the will. The legal certification of validity and a verified copy of the will is mandatory to proceed with carrying it out. Probate, then, is the process of proving the will before a court officer. The court officer may be a judge, a surrogate, a registrar, an officer, or some other legally authorized person who establishes the following:

1. The document is produced for official recognition and registration.
2. It is the last will and testament of the deceased.
3. There are legal formalities in its execution.

The term "testator" means "the deceased." There is no disposition of an estate made, after the testator's death, until the will is probated. The probate of a will is a court proceeding upon notice to the heirs and next of kin. Questions frequently arise about the construction of the terms of a will. The most important rule of construction is that the intention of the testator as it appears from the will shall be carried out whenever legally possible; when the will is ambiguous, the circumstances surrounding its execution may be examined to ascertain the testator's intention.

The statutes as to restrictions on a testator's disposition of his or her property by will differ from state to state. For instance, the degree of participation of the spouse in the estate varies—in many states, a will may not exclude a surviving spouse, whereas in others, it may. Also, many jurisdictions, but not all, permit a person to exclude children from participation in the estate.

The Will

The right to dispose of property by will at death is of ancient origin. Look in the literature of Egypt, Babylon, and Assyria, the Hebrews, the Greeks, and the Romans, and you will find references to wills.

The ancients realized that they could not avoid the inevitable. They made plans for how their wealth and property would be disposed. You, too, cannot avoid the inevitable. Face it! At some time, you will leave this earth. Now is the time for you to determine and state legally how you want your money to be divided among your heirs. Your estate can go to or be divided between your spouse, children (both biological and adopted), grandchildren, or even great-grandchildren. You can leave all or a part to a friend, a niece, a nephew, or to the girl at the restaurant that smiles at you each morning when you come in for a cup of coffee and a roll. You can also remember charities you supported in life and would like to continue supporting in death.

You can also totally disinherit any of these heirs, but, before you do so, you must make these intentions clear. Otherwise, the omitted heirs will be permitted to share on the theory that the omission was accidental rather than purposeful. You can also put them back into your will.

You have the power to make these decisions before your death. This power comes with the writing of your will. As mentioned in the previous paragraph, you also have the power to change your will as things in your life change. Thus, you have the power while you live to avoid making inheritance a nightmare for your family and friends. You avoid this by planning in advance how you want things to be after your death.

The minimum you must do is put your legal documents in order. The number one legal document is your will, drawn up to clearly delineate how you want your assets divided after your death. Many people, unfortunately, do not want to think about their death. As a result, they don't have a plan—that is, a will—to direct the disbursement of their property. (Exhibit A.9 in the appendix is a sample will, provided for your review and study.) You need to work with an attorney to determine what type of will would be appropriate for your specific situation.

Remember: If you don't do it, then the state that you reside in will do it for you. This means that you will not have a say in who gets what. Writing a will can save your estate hundreds, if not thousands, of dollars. In addition, working with an attorney and a financial advisor may avoid the necessity of probate for your estate and help your family enjoy all that you have earned in your lifetime.

A will is one of the most important of all legal documents. There are more legal questions regarding the legality and intention of a will than of any other legal document brought into a courtroom. It becomes imperative that the last declaration of your intentions and desires be legalized so that they are honored and carried out as you directed. In other words, the purpose of a will is to enable an owner of property reasonably to control its disposition after death. The chief purpose of any laws on the subject is to ensure that the true intentions and the wishes of the testator are respected and honored.

The right to make a will depends wholly upon the statutes of the state in which one lives. Most statutes say that every person who is of full age and sound mind, and who owns land, any right in land, or who would be entitled to any interest in land that would be descendible to his or her heirs, could dispose of this property by an instrument called the "last will and testament." The maker (testator) writes out this instrument. The will, handwritten or produced using a word processor and signed in front of witnesses, then becomes a legal document of the maker. It is preferred that two or more witnesses verify the maker's signature. Without a will, the estate would descend to the state (and be referred to as an intestate estate), and debts of the estate would become the property of the state to dispose.

KEY: *Make a will. It will save your family and all those you wanted to provide for after your death headaches and distress.*

TREASURE CHEST

E X E R C I S E

Using the lines below, write a short summary of what you learned as a result of reading this chapter. Make it a point to list at least *three* KEYS in your writing. Indicate clearly how you expect to use these KEYS to guide your financial life.

_____

_____

_____

_____

_____

_____

_____

_____

_____

_____

_____

_____

_____

_____

_____

_____

_____

_____

_____

_____

_____

_____

BRINGING IT ALL TOGETHER

Making the Plan, the Goal, the Dream, into a Reality

In the previous chapters, much content has been covered, yet there is still much to do. You need to make the plan/goal/dream into a reality. It is time for you to put together all that you have learned.

There is much to review, but there are also many new key ideas for you to learn. This chapter will demand yet more commitment from you. However, given what you have already learned, you are more than ready for the activities to come.

Exercise 1: The Text Review

To do this exercise, go through each of the seven chapters in this book and select one idea you found helpful from each chapter. Do *not* use KEYS. There will be another exercise for KEYS. When you complete this exercise, you will have listed seven super ideas you can use to make your financial dreams achievable.

The seven best ideas I received from the chapters are:

Chapter 1 _____

_____

_____

Chapter 2 _____

_____

_____

Chapter 3 _____

_____

_____

Chapter 4 _____

_____

_____

Chapter 5 _____

_____

_____

Chapter 6 _____

_____

_____

Chapter 7 _____

_____

_____

Exercise 2: The KEYS

Now, review the KEYS that appear throughout this text. As with Exercise 1, go through each chapter, but this time select three KEY concepts for each chapter and write them on the appropriate lines that follow. In addition, write a composite statement about how you expect to use those KEYS to achieve your financial goal. Doing this emphasizes that you are responsible for achieving your own financial security, independence, and freedom. **KEY:** *The KEYS can only take you to the door; you must open it.* You have the KEYS to unlock the door.

Chapter 1

KEY _____

KEY _____

KEY _____

I will use each of these KEYS to achieve financial security, independence, and freedom as follows:

_____

_____

_____

_____

_____

_____

Chapter 2

KEY _____

KEY _____

KEY _____

I will use each of these KEYS to achieve financial security, independence, and freedom as follows:

_____

_____

_____

_____

_____

Chapter 3

KEY _____

KEY _____

KEY _____

I will use each of these KEYS to achieve financial security, independence, and freedom as follows:

_____

_____

_____

_____

_____

_____

_____

Chapter 4

KEY _____

KEY _____

KEY _____

I will use each of these KEYS to achieve financial security, independence, and freedom as follows:

_____

_____

_____

_____

_____

_____

_____

Chapter 5

KEY _____

KEY _____

KEY _____

I will use each of these KEYS to achieve financial security, independence, and freedom as follows:

_____

_____

_____

_____

_____

_____

_____

Chapter 6

KEY _____

KEY _____

KEY _____

I will use each of these KEYS to achieve financial security, independence, and freedom as follows:

_____

_____

_____

_____

_____

_____

_____

Chapter 7

KEY _____

KEY _____

KEY _____

I will use each of these KEYS to achieve financial security, independence, and freedom as follows:

_____

_____

_____

_____

_____

_____

Exercise 3 is concerned with your current financial situation. You need to be honest in doing this. The exercise forces you to focus more intently on the achievement of your dream. Exercise 4 deals with how you spend your money. Exercise 5 has to do with what you want to accomplish financially. It is a restatement of the goal you made in Chapter 5.

Exercise 3: My Current Financial Situation

As you have learned, it is imperative that you know your financial situation and budget to be able to plan well. Knowing how much you have and what you owe gives you insight that helps you manage your money more proficiently.

Exhibit 8.1 is a balance sheet for you to complete. Do not go back and look at your figures from before. Instead, fill it out as if this were the first time, avoiding any biases you had when you began using this text. It may be tempting to take a shortcut and copy the exercise you did earlier. In the short run, it will get the exercise done, but in the long run, you will miss the benefit of doing the exercise with accurate numbers. Try not to personalize what you discover. You are still learning how to be financially successful and responsible. There is more to do, and the sheet will assist you in your task.

Now fill in Exhibit 8.1, Assets vs. Debts Balance Sheet.

ASSETS VS. DEBTS BALANCE SHEET.	EXHIBIT 8.1

as of (Date)

ASSETS		LIABILITIES	
Real Estate		Mortgage(s)	
Personal Property		Taxes	
Autos		Operating Expenses	
ACCOUNTS RECEIVABLE		ACCOUNTS PAYABLE	
Cash			
Savings		Insurance Premiums	
Checking			
CDs		Charge Accounts	
Stocks			
Mutual Funds		Loans (payments due others)	
Bonds			
Government Bonds		Installments	
Pension			
Annuity		Credit Cards	
Profit Sharing			
Cash-Value Life Insurance		Other Liabilities	
Loans (payments receivable)			
Other Assets			
TOTAL ASSETS		TOTAL LIABILITIES	
		TOTAL Assets	
		LESS Total Liabilities	
		NET WORTH	

What is your current debt situation? Do you know your debt-to-income ratio? Use Exhibit 8.2, adapted from *The Money Book of Personal Finance* (Eisenberg, 1996), to calculate your current debt status.

EXHIBIT 8.2   CURRENT DEBT STATUS.

Loans and charge accounts:
(Do not list first mortgages or credit cards paid in full each month.)

Last Month's Payments

_____	$ _____
_____	$ _____
_____	$ _____
_____	$ _____
_____	$ _____
_____	$ _____
_____	$ _____
_____	$ _____
_____	$ _____

1. Last month's total payments $ _____
2. Monthly after-tax income $ _____
3. Your debt-to-income ratio $ _____

   Divide line 1 by line 2. This is the percentage of your take-home pay that goes to pay your non-mortgage debt.

4. See the table below to determine if you have too much debt.

	Your Debt-to-Income Ratio			
Your Age	**0–10%**	**10–15%**	**15–20%**	**20%+**
Under 35	A	A	B	C
35–55 (one wage-earner in household)	A	B	C	C
35–55 (two wage-earners in household)	A	A	B	C
Over 55	A	B	C	C

Code Explanation: A = You are doing fine.
                           B = Watch it.
                           C = You are in trouble.

What did you discover about the amount of debt that you are still currently holding? Are you comfortable with your debt-to-income ratio? Would you like to be debt free? It is possible. Others have done it and so can you. Are you willing to become financially secure and debt free?   ❏ Yes   ❏ No I hope you answered "Yes."

Exercise 4A: How I Spend and Manage Money

People who find themselves short of cash often find that the shortage is a result of mismanaging and/or wasting what they have. Small purchases can add up to big expenses. In Exhibit 8.3, identify items that you purchase on a daily, weekly, or monthly basis. Blank spaces are left for you to add specifics that pertain to your own unnecessary expenditures.

Can you see now, how these small expenses steal from the money available for necessary household and personal expenses, and for investing? Your awareness can help you control your unnecessary spending and leave you with more cash.

IDENTIFYING UNNECESSARY EXPENDITURES.			EXHIBIT 8.3
EXPENDITURES	**DAILY EXPENSE**	**WEEKLY EXPENSE**	**MONTHLY EXPENSE**
Eating out			
Snacking			
Movies			
Video rentals			
Cell/telephone			
Morning coffee with donut or other pastry			
Buying clothes on a whim			
ATM fees			
Cigarettes			

Exercise 4B: Finding Missing Money

Now that you are aware of how you waste money, the next part of this exercise focuses on ways of changing your spending behaviors. Answer the questions that follow:

1. Do you *now* believe that you need to change your spending habits?
   ❑ Yes   ❑ No   Why do you think this way?

   _____

   _____

2. Do you think you need to cut back your spending?   ❑ Yes   ❑ No

3. What do you think of cutting back on the expenses identified in Exhibit 8.3?

   _____

   _____

4. What can you cut from your current expenses that will allow you to have more money for paying down debt and investing?

   _____

   _____

5. Once cut, would you use the money saved to pay off debt at a faster rate?   ❑ Yes   ❑ No

6. Once cut, would you use the money saved for investing for retirement?
   ❑ Yes   ❑ No

7. Once cut, would you be willing to use the found money for both?
   ❑ Yes   ❑ No

8. Whose choice is it regarding how you use your money? Explain.

   _____

   _____

   _____

   _____

What choices are you *now* willing to make to turn your plan, goal, and dream into a reality?

Exercise 5: My Financial Goal

Children learn habits from their parents. Therefore, when teenagers have difficulties with money, they usually reflect the patterns of the family. For this reason, I recommend that you make your financial plan a family affair. As I requested for Exercise 3, please do not go back through the text and find your old answers to the questions in this exercise. You need to write fresh answers from scratch. Again, you and your family members must be honest with yourselves.

When you answer the first question, remember to write "I/We plan . . ." or "I/We will . . ." Never say, "I/We will try . . ." A goal is not something that you try to do, but something you *will* do. For instance, a good goal would be "I/we will be out of debt by _____ (date), _____ (month), _____ (year)." Or, "I/we will pay off $4,000 in credit debt by _____ (date), _____ (month), _____ (year)." In my opinion, the best possible goal would be something like: "I/we will cut up *all* credit cards except one, today, _____ (date), _____ (month), _____ (year)."

Financial Goal. My/our financial goal is to: (*If you are doing this exercise with your family, make certain that all members of the family agree with the goal.*)

_____

_____

_____

State clearly what your goal is and when you want to have it achieved. Give yourself a definite date—and even time—that you plan to have it fulfilled. Notice that in the sample goals I gave, a specific date for each goal is given.

Target Date. I/We plan to have my/our financial plan/goal achieved on _____ (day of the week), _____ (date: month/day/year), at _____ (time).

The next section is equally important. It may be what holds you most accountable for achieving your goal. You need to be realistic about this. **KEY:** *Many people in debt are not realistic. They continue to engage in the same debt behavior and fall further into debt.* You now need to state the cost of maintaining the destructive debt behavior.

Consequences of Not Attaining the Financial Goal. (*Be honest with yourself. Admit what the costs and losses would be for you and your family if you do not achieve your financial goal.*)

I/we will experience the following costs and losses if my/our goal is not met:

_____

_____

_____

_____

_____

Can you accept these?   ❑ Yes   ❑ No   (*If this is a real goal, you cannot accept anything less than success in achieving it.*) These negative consequences must never be acceptable to you.

The next item is motivational and should be fun for you to do. It asks what you expect to gain from achieving your financial goal. Some of the results might be: no debt—a big load off your mind, no more phone calls from angry creditors, or having enough cash to pay all your expenses each month and still have money left over for investments, savings, and *fun*. When you achieve your financial goal, the entire world will appear different.

Go ahead and fill in the consequences of your success. You're likely to feel that you know how to accomplish your financial goals and that you are on your way to financial success, independence, and freedom.

Consequences of Attaining the Financial Goal. (*Consider what gains may be in store for you when you achieve your financial goal. Consider only the positive results of getting your finances under control.*) The gains that I/we will experience when we meet my/our financial goal are:

_____

_____

_____

_____

_____

Don't the gains make the financial goal even more desirable?   ❑ Yes   ❑ No

Begin at once to make your financial goal into a reality. Stop making excuses that you are not ready. *Take action today.* A journey of 1,000 miles begins with a single step. *The choice is yours, because you are in charge.*

Appendix

BUDGETS AND OTHER FINANCIAL FORMS

EXHIBIT A.1	ESTIMATED AVERAGE MONTHLY/YEARLY FAMILY EXPENSE BUDGET.

Prepared as of (Date)		
EXPENSE ITEM	**ESTIMATED COST MONTHLY**	**ESTIMATED COST YEARLY**
Housing: Rent/Mortgage	$	$
Car/Transportation	$	$
Health Insurance	$	$
Car Insurance	$	$
Utilities/Cable/Gas/Electric	$	$
Phone/Cell/Fax/Internet Line	$	$
Eating Out	$	$
Clothing	$	$
Food	$	$
Household Items	$	$
Laundry/Dry Cleaning	$	$
Healthcare	$	$
Recreation	$	$
Charges/Credit Cards	$	$
Repairs: Home, Auto, etc.	$	$
Other	$	$
	$	$
	$	$
	$	$
Total	$	$

ASSETS VS. DEBTS BALANCE SHEET.	**EXHIBIT A.2**

as of (Date)			
ASSETS		**LIABILITIES**	
Real Estate		Mortgage(s)	
Personal Property		Taxes	
Autos		Operating Expenses	
ACCOUNTS RECEIVABLE		ACCOUNTS PAYABLE	
Cash			
Savings		Insurance Premiums	
Checking			
CDs		Charge Accounts	
Stocks			
Mutual Funds		Loans (payments due others)	
Bonds			
Government Bonds		Installments	
Pension			
Annuity		Credit Cards	
Profit Sharing			
Cash-Value Life Insurance		Other Liabilities	
Loans (payments receivable)			
Other Assets			
TOTAL ASSETS		TOTAL LIABILITIES	
		TOTAL Assets	
		LESS Total Liabilities	
		NET WORTH	

EXHIBIT A.3   BUDGET WORKSHEET.

CATEGORY	MONTHLY BUDGET AMOUNT	MONTHLY ACTUAL AMOUNT	DIFFERENCE
INCOME: Wages Paid, Misc.			
EXPENSES:			
Rent/Mortgage			
All Utilities			
Cable/Internet/TV			
Telephone			
Home Repairs/Maintenance			
Car Payments			
Gasoline/Oil			
Auto Repairs/Maintenance, Fees, etc.			
Other Transportation Costs			
Auto Insurance			
Child Care			
Home Owners'/Renters' Insurance			
Computer Expenses			
Groceries			
Eating Out			
Credit Cards Expense			
Other			
EXPENSES SUBTOTAL			
NET INCOME (Income Less Expenses)			

Loans and charge accounts:

(Do not list first mortgages or credit cards paid in full each month.)

Last Month's Payments

_____ $ _____

_____ $ _____

_____ $ _____

_____ $ _____

_____ $ _____

_____ $ _____

_____ $ _____

_____ $ _____

_____ $ _____

_____ $ _____

1. Last month's total payments $ _____

2. Monthly after-tax income $ _____

3. Your debt-to-income ratio $ _____

   Divide line 1 by line 2. This is the percentage of your take-home pay that goes to pay your non-mortgage debt.

4. See the table below to determine if you have too much debt.

Your Age	Your Debt-to-Income Ratio			
	0–10%	10–15%	15–20%	20%+
Under 35	A	A	B	C
35–55 (one wage-earner in household)	A	B	C	C
35–55 (two wage-earners in household)	A	A	B	C
Over 55	A	B	C	C

Code Explanation: A = You are doing fine.

                           B = Watch it.

                           C = You are in trouble.

EXHIBIT A.5   ESTIMATED YEARLY HOUSEHOLD OPERATING BUDGET.

Prepared as of (Date) _____ for _____

		Jan.	Feb.	March	April	May	June	July	Aug.	Sept.	Oct.	Nov.	Dec.	Total
Fixed Payments	Total Income													
	Mortgage (rent)													
	Taxes													
	Insurance													
	Loans (payments due to others)													
	Savings													
	Total Fixed Payments													
Flexible Payments	Utilities													
	House Improvements/ Repairs													
	Food													
	Clothing													
	Medical/Dental													
	Education													
	Recreation													
	Magazines/ Newspapers													
	Contributions													
	Automobile Expenditures													
	Credit Charges													
	Other													
	Total Flexible Payments													
Budget	Total Fixed and Flexible Payments													
	Total Income													
	Balance (+ or −)													

SOME MUTUAL FUNDS YOU MAY ENJOY INVESTIGATING.	**EXHIBIT A.6**

Before doing anything, you must carefully study each mutual fund's prospectus.

Publications to study and become familiar with:

Mutual Fund Forecaster—for subscription information	800-442-9000
Money Magazine—for subscription information	800-633-9970
Your Money—for subscription information	800-777-0025

(Each of these publications has a website that you may visit. The sites often include an offer to send you a free copy of their magazine.)

MUTUAL FUND COMPANIES WITH PHONE NUMBERS TO OBTAIN PROSPECTUS

(The listed funds were selected arbitrarily from *Mutual Fund Forecaster* magazine. In addition to calling, you can go to the Internet and learn about each company on its website. I recommend that you study the prospectus before making a commitment to invest money with any of these fund management companies.)

Berger One Hundred	800-333-1001	MFS	800-225-2606
Brandywine	800-656-3017	Mutual Series	800-553-3014
Colonial Small Stock "A"	800-322-2847	Nicholas	414-272-6133
Crabbe Hudson Special	800-541-9732	Oakmark	800-625-6275
Dimensional US 9-10 SM Co	310-395-9005	Putnam	800-225-1581
Fidelity	800-544-8888	Royce	800-221-4268
Franklin	800-342-5236	Strong	800-368-3863
Gabelli	800-422-3554	Templeton	800-292-9293
Janus	800-525-8983	Vanguard	800-662-7447
John Hancock	800-225-5291	Warbas Pincus	800-888-6878
Kaufman	800-237-0132		

Study for at least a year before doing anything. During that year, take at least one financial management seminar. Most colleges and universities offer courses in *financial strategies for successful retirement* and *managing your money 101.*

EXHIBIT A.7 GROCERY STORE COMPARATIVE SHOPPER EXERCISE, SIDE ONE.

Name _____ Week of _____

Store A _____ Store B _____

DAY	SUN		MON		TUES		WED		THURS		FRI		SAT	
DATE														
THE STORE	A	B	A	B	A	B	A	B	A	B	A	B	A	B
GROCERY LIST														
Beverages														
Coffee														
Tea														
Milk														
Cereal														
1.														
2.														
3.														
Freezer—Meat/Veg.														
1.														
2.														
3.														
4.														
Produce														
1.														
2.														
3.														
4.														
Subtotal														
< - > and < + >														
THE STORE	A	B	A	B	A	B	A	B	A	B	A	B	A	B

| | | GROCERY STORE COMPARATIVE SHOPPER EXERCISE, SIDE TWO. | | **EXHIBIT A.7** |

DAY	SUN		MON		TUES		WED		THURS		FRI		SAT	
DATE														
THE STORE	A	B	A	B	A	B	A	B	A	B	A	B	A	B
GROCERY LIST														
Dairy Products														
1.														
2.														
3.														
Laundry Products														
1.														
2.														
3.														
Paper Products														
1.														
2.														
3.														
Desserts														
1.														
2.														
Other														
Other														
Other														
Other														
Subtotal														
< - > and < + >														
THE STORE	A	B	A	B	A	B	A	B	A	B	A	B	A	B

EXHIBIT A.8 — METHOD FOR AVOIDING CREDIT CARD DEBT.

Directions: When you use your credit card, take out your checkbook, and instead of writing a check number in the space, write "CC" in small letters. Record the date and place where you made the charge in the appropriate columns. Subtract the credit card charge from your checking account balance. Keep going! In the Fee column, put a slash mark (/). Wait for the credit card statement to arrive. When it does, go through your checkbook and identify all the CC recordings you have made.

Write out ONE check to your ONE and only credit card company, and under each of the CC notes put the same check number for the one check that you send to cover ALL the charges made. You now have a record of which check you used to pay for each of the charges. Don't double charge yourself. Just write out the check, but do not subtract the amount from the account—you already did that. Last thing to do: In your checkbook over each "/", make a slash going the other way "\". It will look like an "X". This is a quick way to have a record of having paid for these charges.

Ck No.	Date	Transaction Description	Payment/Debit	Code	Fee	Deposit/Credit	Balance

EXTRA COPY

Ck No.	Date	Transaction Description	Payment/Debit	Code	Fee	Deposit/Credit	Balance

EXHIBIT A.9	LAST WILL AND TESTAMENT OF JANE DOE

Be it remembered, that I, JANE DOE, of _____ Street, _____ City, County of _____, State of _____, being of sound mind and memory, do hereby make, execute, and declare this to be my Last Will and Testament.

  I. I will that all my just debts and funeral expenses be paid in full.

  II. I give, devise, and bequeath all the rest, residue, and remainder of my estate to my beloved husband, JOHN DOE.

  III. In the event that my husband, JOHN DOE, does not survive me, or if we should perish in a common accident so that the order of our deaths cannot be determined, I give, devise, and bequeath all of the rest, residue, and remainder of my estate as follows:

    a. To my mother-in-law, JANE SMITH, if she survives me, the sum of $_____

    b. Three-quarters of the rest, residue, and remainder of my estate to the children in equal shares

      _____

      _____

      _____

    c. One quarter of the rest, residue, and the remainder of my estate to National Public Radio.

  IV. I hereby appoint _____ executor of this Will. If she cannot serve, I appoint _____ as executor of this, my Last Will and Testament.

  V. I do hereby revoke all former, any, and every Will heretofore made by me.

Signed _____
JANE DOE

    IN TESTIMONY WHEREOF I have hereunto set my hand and seal this _____ day of _____ 20_____

    WE HEREBY ATTEST that the foregoing instrument was, at the date thereof, in our presence signed, sealed, and declared by JANE DOE, the above named testator, to be her Last Will and Testament, and we at her request, in her presence, and in the presence of each other, did sign our names as witnesses thereto.

_____ residing at _____

_____ residing at _____

_____ residing at _____

REFERENCES

2000 A&E Television Networks. "Biography of William Henry Gates III." [online] http://search.biography.com/print_record.pl?id=15061/ [cited 7 October 2001].

2000 A&E Television Networks. "Biography of Paul S. Allen." [online] www.paulallen.com/profile/biography/ [cited 7 October 2001].

Bottom Line: Personal. (1999–2001).

Burketts, L. "Budgets. Money Matters for Kids." [online] www.mmforkids.org/kids/Kids_budget.htm/ [cited 23 October 2001].

Campbell, D. *If You Don't Know Where You're Going, You'll Probably End Up Somewhere Else* (paperback reissue edition). New York: Thomas More Publishing, 1990.

CCH Business Owner's ToolKit. (2002). Individual Retirement Accounts (IRAs). Retrieved 6/25/02 from www.toolkit.cch.com/text/po8_4820.asp.

Chase. "Investment Planning: Planning for Retirement." [online] www.chase.com/chase/gx.cgi/ [cited 9 October 2001].

CNNMoney on-line. (March 8, 2002). Student debt on the rise. Retrieved 6/25/02 from http://money.cnn.com/2002/03/08/college/q_studentdebt/.

CNNMoney. "Savings Calculator." [online] http://cgi.money.cnn.com/tools/moneygrow/moneygrow_101.html/ [cited 14 October 2001].

Credit Union Land, Inc. "Debt to Income Ratio Calculator." [online] www.culand.com/debt.html/ [cited 23 October 2001].

Eisenberg, R. *The Money Book of Personal Finance.* New York: Money Magazine, 1996.

Ellis, J. and the editors of *Money. Investing for a Secure Retirement.* New York: Money Books, 1995.

Ellis, L. and the editors of *Money. Money Adviser 2000.* New York: Money Books, 2000.

Family Money Magazine (1996–2001).

Fitzgerald, R. "You Can Make a Million." *Reader's Digest,* July 1996, p. 26.

Fleck, C. "Eight tips to beat the swindlers." *NRTA Bulletin,* October 2001, pp. 3, 6.

Goodman, J. E. and Bloch, S. *Everyone's Money Book.* Chicago: Dearborn Financial Publishing, 1994.

Howard, C. "Consumer Advocate." [online] http://clarkhoward.com/ [cited 8 October 2001].

It's Legal. "Wills." [online] www.itslegal.com/infonet/wills/willcat.asp, 2001.

It's Legal. "Wills and Trusts." [online] www.itslegal.com/infonet/wills/Estate1.asp, 2001.

Kehrer, D. *12 Steps to a Worry-Free Retirement.* Washington, DC: Kiplinger Books, 1993.

Konowalow. S. *Cornerstones for Money Management.* Needham Heights, MA: Allyn & Bacon, 1997.

Krandle, R. F. *What everyone should know about wills.* New York: Shelly Publishing, 1979.

Lazarony, L. "Credit cards teaching students a costly lesson." Bankcard.com [online] www.bankrate.com/brm/news/cc/19980605. asp?print+on [cited 5 June 1998].

LegalZoom.com "Wills Library." [online] www.legalzoom.com/law_library/wills/ introduction.html/, 2001.

Lynch, P. *Learn to Earn.* New York: Simon & Schuster, Inc., 1995.

Lynch, P. "Peter Lynch Market Commentary." [online] www.fidelity.com/ [cited 14 October 2001].

Martino, T. "Consumer Advocate." [online] www.troubleshooter.com/ [cited 8 October 2001].

Miller, T. J., Ed. *Invest your way to wealth.* Washington, DC: Kiplinger, 1991.

Modern Maturity. (1999–2002). Refer to a series of articles, as found on www.modernmaturity. org/departments/2002/money/list/html.

Mutual Funds Magazine on-line. "Mutual Funds: The New Rules." [online] www.mutualfunds. com/mfmag/stories/2002/february/retirement/ new_rules_2.html [cited February 2002].

National Education Association. "On the economic status of woman," 1998.

New York Times Direct. "Your Money: The Confidence Game." [online] NYTDirect @nytimes.com/ [cited 15 October 2001].

Owen. D. "Children and Money: Turning Childish Greed into Grown-Up Capitalism." *The Atlantic Monthly Online,* www.the atlantic.com/issues/98apr/kidmoney.htm [cited 23 October 2001].

Patton, N. *Troubleshooter.com. Las Vegas Review–Journal,* January 11, 2002, p. 1B.

Ramsey, D. *Financial Peace.* New York: Viking Group, 1997.

Respond.com. "Wills and Probate." [online] www.respond.com/buyers/requestform.jsp?no proxy=1&cat=1700000085&path=17000000 78&bd=11&src=12151&db=1/, 2001.

Scudder Investor Services, Inc. *Investing: The Basics.* Boston, MA, 1997.

Schwab, C. *The Essential Investor: Special Retirement Edition.* San Francisco, CA: Schwab, 1996.

Sherfield, R., Montgomery, R. and Moody, P. *Cornerstone: Building on Your Best, Third Edition.* Upper Saddle River, NJ: Prentice Hall, 2002.

Social Security Administration. *What every woman should know.* SSA Publication No. 05-10127, October 1999.

Social Security Administration. *What you need to know when you get retirement or survivors benefits.* SSA Publication No. 05-10077, May 2000.

Stanley, T. J., and Danko, W. D. *The Millionaire Next Door.* Atlanta: Longstreet Press, 1997.

Tanous, P., and Tobias, R. C. *Investment Gurus: A Road Map to Wealth from the World's Best Money Managers.* Upper Saddle River, NJ: Prentice Hall, 1996.

Terrell, B. (2002). "Top Ten Student Money Mistakes." *Young Money,* August.

U. S. News & World Report, Inc. *Complete family financial record book,* 1997.

U. S. Department of Commerce, Bureau of the Census. "Income in 1999 by Educational Attainment for People 25 Years Old and Over: March 2000." [online] www.census.gov/main/www/cen2000.html [cited 9 October 2001].

U. S. Department of Education. *Student Financial Assistance. Funding your Education 2001/2002,* 2001.

INDEX